# The Superwoman Myth

I0130412

The book begins by raising a thoughtful question, "Can women have it all, family, work and everything in between?" If yes, then are women 'super-women'? More importantly, what or who is a 'superwoman'? In other words, this book discusses the role of contemporary women in today's modern career world and its myriad of challenges, and in turn explores the nuanced role of millennial women and provides insights into how women juggle demands at home and at work; family and career management.

Using case studies from interviews with two hundred women, the authors draw on data from women themselves to explore how they navigate their daily lives to achieve work-life balance. This book will motivate readers to reframe their roles at home and in the workplace and hopefully help them reclaim control in their career/family journeys. This book is also an essential guide to thought leadership for women in leadership positions or aspiring to be in leadership positions. Finally, this book will demystify gender roles in the workplace and at home, enabling women of all ages and backgrounds to embark on their career with confidence.

This book will motivate younger women who are embarking on their first career and looking to develop the inner leadership that helps them thrive in life.

**Jennifer Loh** is an Associate Professor in Management, Deputy Head of School (DHoS), and the Associate Dean, Research (Higher Degree by Research) at Canberra Business School (University of Canberra), Australia.

**Raechel Johns** is the Head of the Canberra Business School at the University of Canberra, Australia.

**Rebecca English** is a Senior Lecturer in the School of Teacher Education and Leadership, Queensland University of Technology, Australia.

"It's been some decades since 'You can't have it all' became 'Girls can do anything!', but as this new book makes crystal clear, the reality for contemporary women has not significantly changed from that of our mothers. We are in the midst of one of the great technological transformations, and as the authors show, now is a fine time to craft new paths that might bridge that tired old gender divide. Mixing personal stories with national statistics, they offer an informed and accessible account of the past and present, and of possible futures that are woven through with strands of optimism. Whether considering the gig economy, intersectional identities, educational options, women's rights or political constraints, they illuminate the bollards and the bypasses that characterize the twenty-first century context for women as a group, as a congress of separate groups, and as economic and political actors in the current world."

— ***Distinguished Professor Jen Webb***, *Dean,*
*Graduate Research (University of Canberra),*
*Distinguished Professor of Creative Practice*

# The Superwoman Myth

Can Contemporary Women Have It All Now?

**Jennifer Loh, Raechel Johns and Rebecca English**

Routledge
Taylor & Francis Group

LONDON AND NEW YORK

First published 2022
by Routledge
2 Park Square, Milton Park, Abingdon, Oxon OX14 4RN

and by Routledge
605 Third Avenue, New York, NY 10158

*Routledge is an imprint of the Taylor & Francis Group, an informa business*

*British Library Cataloguing-in-Publication Data*
A catalogue record for this book is available from the British Library

*Library of Congress Cataloging-in-Publication Data*
Names: Loh, Jennifer, author. | Johns, Raechel, 1976- author. | English, Rebecca, 1977- author.
Title: The superwoman myth : can contemporary women have it all now? / Jennifer Loh, Raechel Johns, Rebecca English.
Other titles: Super woman myth
Description: Milton Park, Abingdon, Oxon ; New York, NY : Routledge, 2022. | Includes bibliographical references and index. |
Identifiers: LCCN 2021038248 (print) | LCCN 2021038249 (ebook) | ISBN 9780367896911 (hardback) | ISBN 9780367896928 (paperback) | ISBN 9781003020554 (ebook)
Subjects: LCSH: Women—Social conditions. | Women—Psychology. | Work and family. | Leadership in women. | Work-life balance.
Classification: LCC HQ1155 .L64 2022 (print) | LCC HQ1155 (ebook) | DDC 305.42—dc23
LC record available at https://lccn.loc.gov/2021038248
LC ebook record available at https://lccn.loc.gov/2021038249

ISBN: 9780367896911 (hbk)
ISBN: 9780367896928 (pbk)
ISBN: 9781003020554 (ebk)

DOI: 10.4324/9781003020554

Typeset in Times New Roman
by codeMantra

*We dedicate this book to all the "superwomen" in our lives who have encouraged us in our pursuit of our dreams. They have been a constant source of inspiration: So, let us continue the fight because everything starts with a dream!*

# Contents

# Illustrations

## Figures

## Tables

# Introduction – the motivations behind this book

We all had slightly different motivations for writing this book, but one of the things that was important to us all was to understand what a 'superwoman' means in today's contemporary world especially for inspiring career women, and why women are feeling increasingly pulled in a million directions. We also wanted to know if being a 'superwoman' is even something that women should be aspiring for. And we wanted some solutions for the juggle that women tend to experience in their day to day life. We wanted to address leadership, and the importance of women stepping up if they choose to, to advance their careers. But we also wanted to acknowledge that is not a choice everyone wishes to make. Some women are happy in their jobs and careers as they are, without constantly striving. Some wish to reduce their work commitments, after years of investing in their work. And others prefer to stay at home, raising children, or focusing on hobbies.

## Superwoman: it is a woman's issue

In other words, we wanted this book to be as representative as possible. We wanted you to read it and nod along with some of the examples, seeing your situation. We put a call out for women to talk to and were surprised to hear from over 200 women. It was challenging to write a book about women without reverting to stereotypes, and we worried, the whole time we were writing this book, that there will be unbalanced views. We have strived very hard to make sure we have shared diverse examples in this book. Therefore, we have included stories from women with or without children, to women with or without partners, or even women with more than one partner. We interviewed Australian women with different multicultural backgrounds, we spoke with women in heterosexual relationships, and those in same-sex relationships. We have included data on gender non-binary and transgender people, too, as well as highlighted the experiences of First Nations women and people from other cultural backgrounds. But, despite our efforts to be representative, we do have many examples that are skewed more towards partnered women, and women with children. No matter how balanced we want to be, when we talk about the mental load, and the juggle, it is women

DOI: 10.4324/9781003020554-1

with children who seem to feel it strikes a chord most of all and step forward to share their stories. This does not mean that there is not a juggle for those managing career + relationship, career + parenting, career + life, generally or even just life, minus career – of course. There is a juggle, but women with children were keener to chat to us. The majority of our respondents were partnered women with children, but we've made sure to share many other examples too, because we know that women without children, and single women, also have to tackle the mental load just as much as partnered women with children do. It is a women's issue, not a mother's issue.

While the three of us, as authors, are academics, we come from diverse backgrounds and experiences, and that influenced our motivation to write this book.

### Jennifer's motivations

One of us is a migrant woman who now calls Australia home. She met her husband in university, and they were married after a decade of dating. She came to motherhood rather late having decided to prioritise her career. She always knew that she would continue working even after her son was born. She has always believed that she can be both a mother and a career woman. Isn't that what every modern woman wants, to be a 'superwoman'? Her primary motivation to write this book came from her son. When her son was 3 months old, she decided to leave him at the childcare centre. Many mothers in her mother's group thought that was too soon. When her son was about 6 years old, he asked her why she rushed around so much every day? She remembered dismissing her son's question. Why? Well, because she was in the middle of getting him ready for school and herself off to work. But that night when she finally has some time to herself (of course, after finishing the cooking, washing, and a final check on work emails), she has a real good think about her son's question. She was unable to come up with an answer, well, not a convincing enough answer for herself. Are other women rushing about in their daily lives? Do other women feel out of breath all the time? What makes a good mother? What makes a good career woman? How do other women cope with work and household chores? Those questions became the driving force behind the research questions for this book. She also discovered that the ideal of being a 'superwoman' is fraught with micro- and macro-expectations; expectations that come from not only one's society and culture but also from other men and women. Ultimately, she believes that as women, we should have the freedom to make our own decisions and on our own terms. Only and only then, can women be truly free and super.

### Raechel's motivations

One of us is in a same-sex relationship, and she and her partner have children together. Her main motivation to write this book was two-fold – first, she absolutely loves reading media commentary, perspectives, and academic research on the juggle/mental load/doing it all and leadership. As a Business academic, contributing to this discussion was something she was really interested in. But, also, as someone in a same-sex relationship, she is a little astounded by how outdated the perspectives on this debate seems. Surely, we have moved on by now! There are plenty of stay-at-home dads with career mum partners and aren't men doing more at home? The stats tell us that. Except, we have not really moved on, at least when it comes to the mental load. To her, it is simple – partners just need to discuss which tasks they like, and do not like, what they have time for, and allocate responsibilities. However, it seems it is not as simple as that in a heterosexual relationship, and this was something she wanted to explore and even in same-sex relationships, there can still be one person carrying the mental load more so than the other. Our research incorporated in this book shows that, often, the debate continues, regardless of situation. Other situations – like single parents, stay-at-home mums, and couples without children – all come with their own unique situations, and that is something we have also incorporated into this book.

## Rebecca's motivations

One of us is in a traditional marriage, with three children. She and her husband met at school, got married shortly after and stayed together. Her main motivation to write this book was its place in her own work focused on how parents, mothers, in particular, decide on an education for their children which accords with their beliefs about good parenting. After becoming a teacher, and working in school marketing, she became acutely aware of the kind of mental load women carry in families where they have children. Her interest in this topic comes from the immense respect she developed, as a 20 something early teacher who was trying to appeal to parents. The schools she taught in were the kinds of schools that were considered 'tough'. Understanding how different experiences affect young people's life chances, and how those life chances reverberate down the generational lines is something that has always been a feature of her working life. She holds immense respect for the work mothers do every day, particularly mothers who became mothers as very young women or mothers who have to make sacrifices whether that's single mothers, mothers who escape domestic and family violence, and mothers who homeschool because of problems in schools.

It is important to understand that every woman has their own unique story. We cannot possibly tell them all. We have, however, aimed to be as representative as possible, hoping that you will see friends and family, and maybe yourself, in some of the examples, and in reflecting on solutions proposed, they may spark ideas for you. We have also included a chapter on diversity, as a way of acknowledging differences between us all.

**What about you?**

As women, we are not alone. Although the specifics of our lives and situations differ, we are not alone in our daily struggles, be it in the workplace, in society, at home, or with our partners. Through the diverse stories we share of women from different cultures, backgrounds, and walks of life, we have endeavoured to share women's voices. This collective voice is not just about expressing our frustration, it is also about speaking up and determining a way forward for greater equality at home and at work. We hope women can embrace and empathise with each other, to encourage and to support other women's choices and decisions. We have also shared some women's strategies for dealing with stress, in addition to ideas around upskilling to be ready for the changing workplace and making the workplace more equitable. We encourage you to start a conversation about the topics you find in this book, to explore strategies you can implement, and changes you can make in the community. Let's share our knowledge and dreams with each other and – build a more just and equitable world for all.

# 1 Becoming 'superwoman' or not?

Women everywhere are always expected to continually imagine what one situation, or another would look like from a male point of view. Men are almost never expected to do the same for women. So deeply internalised is this pattern of behaviour that many men react to any suggestion that they might do otherwise as if it were itself an act of violence.

David Graeber (2009) *The Utopia of rules*

When we were at high school in the 1990s, the teachers used to give out long bumper stickers that said, "girls can do anything". It was a different time. On demand vinyl stickers were yet to be invented. Nobody was making "well behaved women rarely make history" t-shirts yet and while we would all have studied Shakespeare and had all recited Helena's line from A Midsummer Night's Dream, "and though she be but little, she is fierce", nobody was making toddler hoodies with the phrase. We took our "girls can do anything" stickers and stuck them to the bottom of our school bags, with a rhetorical flourish of putting them on an angle. Interestingly, the boys would often comment on how they did not get such a sticker, and how come they only make those types of things for girls?

Those stickers were given out at some inspirational soiree, or some leadership seminar or some pastoral care event that included speakers who told us how amazing it was to be a girl. How we had the world at our feet. These events, and the stickers, also came with a haughty lecture about standing on our own 2 feet, being flexible, adaptable, and independent. The messaging was heavy on the idea that women were equal to men, that we did not have to feel constrained by our sex or our gender.

Girls can do anything is pretty much a metaphor for how women have been raised since the 1990s. Cultural products from She-Ra to SheZow made it clear that women and girls can have it all, can do it all, can be anything. The messages tried to cover all bases. Girls did not have to be teachers or nurses – but they could be if they wanted to be. Girls did not have to be mothers, but they could be if they wanted to be. Girls did not have to shy away from engineering or medicine, but she should not feel forced to, if she

DOI: 10.4324/9781003020554-2

did not want to. However, it does not take much to realise the 'anything' in that sticker is actually a synonym for 'everything'. We were meant to think we could do it all, do everything, which sold us on an idea that to be a successful woman, we had to have it all, to be it all, to do it all. Many women have interpreted that message to mean we have to do everything all the time. That we could simultaneously be successful mothers and successful career women. We could have children – two/three/five – as many as we wanted, whenever we wanted, without a man if we wanted and snap right back to who we were before those kids came along physically, mentally, and in terms of our careers. Much of the 'girls can do anything/everything' message was that we should be wanting to crack glass ceilings and make our way into the upper echelons of business, of Science, Technology, Engineering, and Mathematics (STEM), of community, of politics, of education, and of society.

But, these stickers, and these ideas, leave a lot of questions. For instance, what does it mean to do anything? What about those girls who did not want to do everything? What about those girls who really wanted what their grandmothers had? A nice family, a nice house, and had no real ambitions towards upper echelons or breaking glass ceilings? Where did they fit in the 'girls can do anything and everything' messaging?

The other point that we are sure many of you reading this have thought about is, of course, the pressure to be everything falls on women. On us. We have to do all the change making to make our own anything happen. It responsibilised us – girls and women – to be 'superwomen'. It became our responsibility to make a change that the world needed, rather than asking, why is the world like this? What barriers are there that prevented women in the past from doing everything? Can we really do anything when the world is so unequal? In this book, we are on a journey to find out.

This book is about 'superwomen'.

Or, more precisely, this book is about what it means to be a late capitalist 'superwoman' in the contemporary Western world. It is about who has it all and who does not. It is about what happens to women who try to have it all, and what happens to women who do not care to have it all. Using personal stories shared with us by the many women we talked to and contemporary examples, this book explores the work/life reality many women face. Really, this book is about what it means to be a woman in the contemporary Western world. Let us start by thinking about what this world looks like for women.

## Contemporary lives of women

Women's lives are changing, and fast. While we are having fewer babies, we are working longer hours at work while simultaneously doing more housework in our homes (Australian Institute of Family Studies – AIFS, 2020). In 2019, women worked more hours than they had in any other time in history. In Australia, for example, in the 1980s, less than 60% of partnered mothers

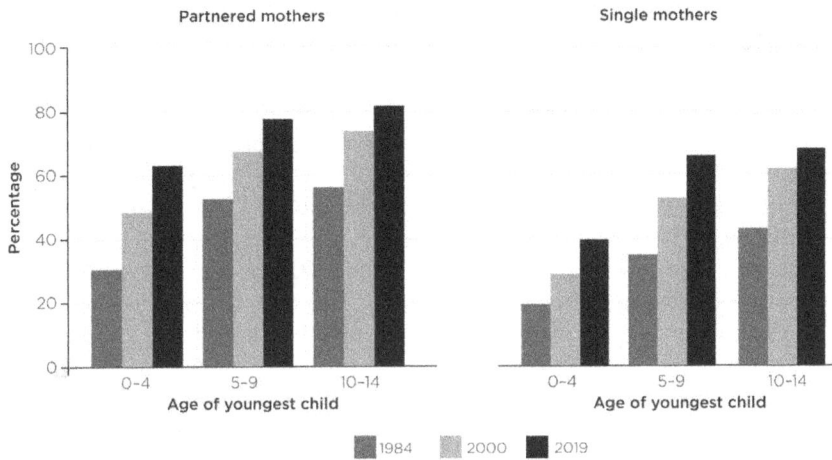

*Figure 1.1* How we worked.
Source: Australian Bureau of Statistics with credit to Australian Institute of Family Studies.

worked when they had children in the 10–14 age group, by 2019, that figure was over 80%. Interestingly, but perhaps unsurprisingly, single mothers
worked fewer hours than their partnered sisters. Figure 1.1 taken from the
Australian Institute of Family Studies report, "How we Worked", illustrate
these points.

An interesting fact about women's workforce participation includes that
attitudes towards women's employment, particularly after they become
partnered or mothers, have changed significantly since 2000. For example,
attitudes towards women working because they enjoy their work, rather
than "needing the money", has resulted in greater support. The judgement
around the impact on the children by having working mothers has also softened. Nearly 60% of Australian Bureau of Statistics respondents agreed
that women can still have as good a relationship with her children if she
works or if she does not. Similarly, they softened their beliefs about whether
women should work if they are okay financially, from nearly 40% in the early
2000s to only about 20% in 2015 (AIFS, 2020).

Another interesting statistic in that data set was the attitude to mothering. While, in 2001, nearly 80% agreed that the most important role a
woman has is being a mother, regardless of career, this decreased to nearly
70% by 2015. Perhaps the view that a women's primary role in life is being
a mother has shifted, but only very slightly. These data suggest that women
are still really encouraged to be parents! However, we'd hasten to add that
almost the exact same percentages were seen in response to the question
about whether a man's primary role in life is to be a father, so perhaps it is
not just women under pressure to be parents.

**BOX 1.1 BEC'S STORY – MEMORIES OF SUPERWOMEN PAST**

When I was in high school, I told my grandmother I had to write an essay for Modern History. It was about the rise of the Chinese Communist Party. I told my grandmother I had this essay to write and rolled my eyes like a normal 15 years old and said I was not particularly interested. She was not at all pleased. She reminded me how modern it was in history for women to have the opportunity to go to school, to do secondary level studies, and to have the opportunity to go to university. She was angry that I failed to appreciate the good fortune of having a weekend assignment to write 900 words on Mao Zedong and the rise of the modern Chinese Communist Party. She told me she would have loved to write that assignment; it would have been a real opportunity to learn to craft an argument and learn about our region. I remember thinking she was high or boring or something, and I failed to appreciate the meaning behind her exhortations to me to enjoy the experience.

My grandmother was born into a London slum in Hammersmith in the early 1910s, the oldest of six surviving children. She was desperate to have an education but, being a girl and living in tenement housing with parents who were not educated or wealthy, that was unlikely. Her father fought in the First World War, sustained some injuries that eventually killed him, but not before he and my great grandmother had had a few more children. Her whole family, my grandmother's parents and her five siblings, lived in one room. She washed the family's clothes on the stairs with a bucket of water they collected from a pump on the street. Her sister told me how they had perfected washing on the stairs without taking all their clothes off. It was a tough life. But, it was not enough for my grandmother.

She decided, in her late teens, she would take elocution lessons. Keenly aware of how social class was destiny in London in the 1920s and 1930s, she worked and spent her spare money on learning to speak English like a lady. She worked hard, met my grandfather and, after a time and just before the Second World War broke out, they left England for Australia and got married. Nobody knew where she had come from and she prevented contact from her relations in the case it became clear she was not quite the lady she had always wanted to be and to which she had always aspired.

I guess that is why she was so keen to do my modern history assignment, or at least to have me do it. She understood the restrictive roles women in the past had been forced into and the ways that fates outside of women's control kept them in their homes and out of the workforce.

I did not understand it at the time, and her history was pieced together from stories told by her much younger sisters, but her desire for me to do a good job on my Mao Zedong assignment (I did not by the way, I remember not wanting to do it and only doing a half-baked job) was more about her desire to have had all the opportunities she saw her grandchildren having than to do an actual assignment on the Chinese Communist Party.

## History of education for women

Most people believe there was a time when women did not get much educating. It seemed pointless to waste money on an education when the woman would have a man to rely on and, outside of reading and writing, would not need much of an education (Thorpe, 2017). Women's education has always been a class issue, with those who were better off – the wealthy families – having money to spend on educating women. Sometimes this education was only in finishing schools so they would be, not only good wives and mothers but also reasonable and companionable women for the betterment of their husbands and society at large (Kelley, 2006). However, the fight for post-compulsory education was long and arduous. Many women saw the only way to get any kind of decent, higher level role (remembering these were frequently times where if you have got to the equivalent of Grade 3 you'd been extremely well educated), was through a nunnery (Thorpe, 2017). The nineteenth century saw a real improvement in women's education, with a women's college, Girton, being established at Cambridge and co-ed Oberlin College at University College London. However, that improvement was only for white women and, as the colleges they attended in the UK suggest, posh or wealthy women. Poor women, especially women of colour had to wait until the 1960s and 1970s with second wave feminism to get a look into traditionally white institutions in the USA. It is even worse at the top, with Oxford appointing its first female Vice Chancellor (or head of the institution) in the mid-2010s. Women still only make up about 30% of all VCs in the USA and the UK. Australia is not any better, neither is New Zealand. But these statistics are good compared to the global south where, take South Africa as an example, it is only 15% of VCs who are women (Macupe, 2020).

Significantly, while education may have changed for women, and women's rights at work have been improved, we have not really experienced many gains in housework, in their caring responsibilities and in their incomes (Burkeman, 2018). Women still do the majority of the housework, and Nicole Batemen and Martha Ross (2020) from The Brookings Institute reported that during the COVID-19 lockdowns across the world, women found themselves doing more of the caring responsibilities than their partners. Unlike the 2008 financial crash, the current economic impact has affected many women who are now jobless (McKinsey & Co, 2021). In addition to the gaps women traditionally take to care for children and elderly relatives, women were suddenly taking an unanticipated gap in their work due to redundancies.

**Pay gaps and time out**

One of the ways that women's rights at work have changed is in terms of their ability to take a legal break to have children. Although the USA is an exception, most other liberal, democratic, social capitalistic countries allow women to have a paid break from the workforce when they have a child. These countries not only guarantee a women's job while on maternity leave but also pay them some or all of their wage while they are on maternity leave. Some countries, principally Nordic countries, also offer men the same benefits and encourage them to take a similar break when they become fathers.

However, the insidious problem of women not being equal in the workplace remains. It may be that the high rates of women working part time, as we will talk about in relation to company directorships below, particularly after they have children, is a part of the reason why they are not equal in the workplace. It may lead to the problem that manifests in women not making it to the top echelons of workplaces.

The Australian Workplace Gender and Equality Agency (2021) data show that women's share of senior management is still far from representative. Women hold only 15% of chair positions, only 28% of directorships, and only 18% of CEOs in Australia are female. These data are in spite of the rises in employment of women where nearly 50% of the workforce is female. It may be that, as the same data set shows, women are nearly 70% of the part-time employee workforce, and that may impact on their rise to the top. But, things are changing. Real-time data from the Australian Institute of Company Directors (2020) reporting on data from 2020 show that around 30% of all ASX organisations are headed by women. So, there is some hope for improvement.

However, the high rates of part-time employment and the gaps in working that many women take to have children manifest in many ways. The problem is especially stark when looking at the rates of women's poverty in old age. Women are, on average, 100,000 in the hole on their male counterparts at retirement age, according to Q-Super, and a peak lobby group, Women in Super, showing that they have roughly half the superannuation of men and live on average an extra five years. These data leave women in a more precarious position, relying heavily on the aged pension in older age. Around a third of women aged over 60 are living in poverty (Heath, 2017), in part due to an average of six years break women take in their careers due to childbirth which creates a nearly $80,000 drop in superannuation savings (Women in Super), which means they can't retire when they want to or are not able to end working in their 60s. These data suggest that life's challenges, such as job loss, divorce, or experiencing domestic violence and abuse can all exacerbate this condition for women. Women are also increasing in homelessness statistics, with Australian Health and Welfare reporting in 2020 that 60% of clients who access homeless services are women (AIHW, 2020, Q-super, 2021; Women in super, 2021)

## Mothers who work and working mothers

With increasing rates of women in the workforce, to anyone born between the late 1970s and the 1990s, it seems like more and more women work now than they did when we were children. And many more of those women are mothers. This age group is one which we, the authors, fall in, and perhaps you do, too. As a generation, we seem to work more hours than our mothers did, continue in our professions in a way many of our mothers could never have dreamed of, and have more rights at work than they did. We seem to be more interested in a work/life balance and in trying to make a career work with child rearing responsibilities, regardless of whether we work full time or part time. While, yes, most of us will remember the latch-key kids who went home to empty houses each afternoon, it seemed they were a minority. We remember teachers pitying those poor waifs who had to do their homework on their own because their mothers, heaven forbid, were working. It was always the mother who was criticised for not being there, never the father, and it was always the mother onto whose shoulders fell the burden of care, including ensuring homework was up to scratch, uniforms looked clean and tidy, and lunches were healthy and filling.

Anyone born in the late 1970s may have had the experience of their mother having to quit her job due to employment law at the time. There was not a choice. It was not because a woman felt it was right to be there to collect her children from school or open the door for them when they walked back home. It was not even a moral decision about the rights and responsibilities for children's rearing and welfare. Many women in that age group had to quit their employment because employment law said you could not be simultaneously employed and pregnant. In the USA, it only became illegal to fire an employee for being pregnant in 1978 (Kurtz, 2014). Those women did better than others who are slightly older who had had to quit their jobs when they got married. By the 1980s though, things were changing and more and more mothers were working. But, the statistics above showing women's working changes haven't impacted on their expectations at home suggest maybe it's not all good news.

A significant part of this employment story is childcare. The reason more mothers are able to work now than 40 years ago is because childcare is more readily available. While mothers and sisters who did not work were frequently called upon to undertake the childcare in the past, women relied on their mothers and their sisters because there were no other, paid, options. Childcare, as a paid and formalised service option, really began in the 1980s after the Australian parliament got involved in the early 1970s which led, in the early to mid-1980s, to the establishment of more than 6,000 day-care places in Australia (Australian Parliament House – APH, 1997). These women needed someone to care for children before they were at school, so they could resume their jobs and careers without the massive penalty their mothers, if they had been lucky enough to be able to work, had endured. Childcare has been a major element in revolutionising the world of work for women.

## Sisters are doing it for themselves

All the while, there is a change in the ways families were structured. Any-one born before the 1980s would struggle to know someone who have had a parent divorce. They did, of course, but it just was not something you talked about. Teachers at school would console you if you were a child of a 'broken home'. It was something embarrassing. We remember in the 1980s even the talk about so-and-so in our primary schools whose parents had gotten divorced. It was a source of shame. A point of difference. However, as norms changed, and more and more families experienced this phenomenon, it became normalised. Same sex-families, and their increasing visibility in the general population, also affect how families are viewed. Australian data suggest that, since first asking about same-sex couples on the census in 1996, there has been a rise of 32% of households identifying as same-sex since then. Of those couples, 52% were male and 48% female and roughly 12% had children living with them (Qu, Knight & Higgins, 2016).

Table 1.1 shows just how much families (with children) are changing. It's drawn from a 2011 Organisation for Economic Co-operation and Development – OECD report titled "Doing better for families" (p. 28).

*Table 1.1* Distribution of children[1] by household type, selected OECD countries, 2007

| | Percentage of children living with: | | | | | % of children in multigenerational households |
|---|---|---|---|---|---|---|
| | *0 parents* | *1 parent* | *2 cohabiting parents* | *2 married parents* | *Total* | |
| Australia | 2.6 | 16.8 | 81.0 | | 100 | : |
| Austria | 2.2 | 14.3 | 7.4 | 76.1 | 100 | 7.5 |
| Belgium | 2.5 | 16.2 | 13.7 | 67.7 | 100 | 2.2 |
| Canada | 0.0 | 22.1 | 11.0 | 66.9 | 100 | : |
| Czech Republic | 0.6 | 14.9 | 8.2 | 76.3 | 100 | 7.7 |
| Denmark | 1.5 | 17.9 | 15.1 | 65.6 | 100 | 0.4 |
| Estonia | 1.9 | 21.8 | 23.9 | 52.5 | 100 | 12.0 |
| Finland | 0.9 | 14.4 | 15.8 | 68.9 | 100 | 0.6 |
| France | 0.9 | 13.5 | 21.0 | 64.5 | 100 | 1.8 |
| Germany | 1.3 | 15.0 | 5.5 | 78.2 | 100 | 0.9 |
| Greece | 1.2 | 5.3 | 1.2 | 92.3 | 100 | 6.5 |
| Hungary | 0.8 | 15.4 | 9.9 | 73.9 | 100 | 11.6 |

| | | | | | | |
|---|---|---|---|---|---|---|
| Ireland | 1.9 | 24.3 | 5.9 | 67.9 | 100 | 4.5 |
| Italy | 0.8 | 10.2 | 5.2 | 83.9 | 100 | 5.0 |
| Japan | 0.0 | 12.3 | 87.7 | | 100 | : |
| Luxembourg | 0.3 | 10.2 | 6.9 | 82.6 | 100 | 2.8 |
| Netherlands | 0.3 | 11.1 | 13.1 | 75.5 | 100 | 0.3 |
| New Zealand | 0.0 | 23.7 | 76.3 | | 100 | : |
| Poland | 0.8 | 11.0 | 9.2 | 79.0 | 100 | 22.0 |
| Portugal | 2.9 | 11.9 | 9.7 | 75.5 | 100 | 11.6 |
| Slovak Republic | 1.1 | 10.6 | 3.7 | 84.7 | 100 | 17.6 |
| Slovenia | 0.6 | 10.4 | 19.5 | 69.4 | 100 | 13.7 |
| Spain | 1.2 | 7.2 | 7.9 | 83.7 | 100 | 5.8 |
| Sweden | 1.3 | 17.6 | 30.5 | 50.6 | 100 | 0.3 |
| Switzerland | 0.1 | 15.2 | 84.7 | | 100 | : |
| United Kingdom | 1.4 | 21.5 | 12.6 | 64.5 | 100 | 3.4 |
| United States | 3.5 | 25.8 | 2.9 | 67.8 | 100 | : |
| **OECD27 average** | **1.3** | **14.9** | **11.3** | **72.5** | **100.0** | **6.6** |

Source: Iacovou and Skew (2010), *Household Structure in the EU.*
*Notes*: The category "2 cohabiting parents" includes unmarried parents and parents in reconstituted households.
Data missing for Chile, Iceland, Israel, Korea, Mexico, Norway and Turkey.
1  Children are defined as household members aged under 18; <15 for Canada and New Zealand.: means close to 0 and is negligible.

## Where to from here?

In the following chapters of this book, we will share diverse stories and life experiences of women from different cultures, races, and backgrounds. These life stories open us to the vast and diverse challenges but also joy of being a contemporary, twenty-first century women. These women have dreams and many worked hard to pursue their dreams in an often masculine world. This book and its chapters are about women and their voices. We hope when you've finished reading all the chapters in this book, you not only hear their voices but also their roars. We also hope when you've finished reading this book, you feel inspired to tackle the challenges in your life, but also better support the women around you.

We hope that, like the bumper stickers, you think 'women can do anything (they choose to do)'.

## Reference list

Australian Institute of Company Directors (2020, November 18). More than a third of ASX200 boards still at less than 30 per cent women. Retrieved from https://aicd.companydirectors.com.au/media/media-releases/more-than-a-third-of-asx200-boards-still-at-less-than--30-per-cent-women

Australian Institute of Family Studies (2020). How we worked. Retrieved from https://apo.org.au/sites/default/files/resource-files/2020-08/apo-nid307568.pdf.

Australian Institute of Health and Welfare (AIHW) (2020, December 11). Homelessness and homelessness services. Retrieved from https://www.aihw.gov.au/reports/australias-welfare/homelessness-and-homelessness-services.

Australian Parliament House (APH, 1997). Childcare in Australia: Current provision and recent developments. Retrieved from https://www.aph.gov.au/About_Parliament/Parliamentary_Departments/Parliamentary_Library/Publications_Archive/Background_Papers/bp9798/98bp09#DEVELOPMENT.

Australian Workplace Gender and Equality Agency (2021). Australia's Gender Pay Gap Statistics. Retrieved from https://www.wgea.gov.au/publications/australias-gender-pay-gap-statistics

Bateman, N., & Ross, R. (2020, October). Why has COVID-19 been especially harmful to working women? Retrieved from https://www.brookings.edu/essay/why-has-covid-19-been-especially-harmful-for-working-women/.

Burkeman, O. (2018, February 17). Dirty secret: Why is there still a housework gender gap? Retrieved https://www.theguardian.com/inequality/2018/feb/17/dirty-secret-why-housework-gender-gap.

Graeber, D. (2015). *The utopia of rules: On technology, stupidity, and the secret joys of bureaucracy.* Brooklyn, NY: Melville House.

Heath, N. (2017, December 5). Aged over 60 and female? Here's why you might be at risk of poverty. Retrieved from https://www.sbs.com.au/topics/voices/culture/article/2017/11/24/aged-over-60-and-female-heres-why-you-might-be-risk-poverty#:~:text=When%20it%20comes%20to%20finances,in%20Australia%20live%20in%20poverty.%22.

Iacovou, M., & Skew, A.J. (2010). Household structure in the EU. ISER working paper series 2010–10, Institute for Social and Economic Research.

Kelley, M. (2006). *Learning to stand and speak: Women, education, and public life in America's Republic* (p. 312). Chapel Hill: Omohundro Institute, University of North Carolina Press. ISBN 0-8078-3064-2 (cl).

Kurtz, A. (2014, July 28). 8 rights of pregnant women at work. Retrieved from https://money.cnn.com/2014/07/25/news/economy/rights-pregnant-workers/index.html.

Macupe, B. (2020, August 20). Few women leaders in academia. Retrieved from https://mg.co.za/education/2020-08-20-few-women-leaders-in-academia/.

McKinsey and Co (2021, March 8). Seven charts that show COVID-19's impact on women's employment. Retrieved from https://www.mckinsey.com/featured-insights/diversity-and-inclusion/seven-charts-that-show-covid-19s-impact-on-womens-employment.

Organisation for Economic Co-operation and Development (OECD, 2011). Doing better for families. Retrieved from http://dx.doi.org/10.1787/888932393958.

Q-Super (2021). How much super should I have at my age? Retrieved from https://qsuper.qld.gov.au/super/how-much-super-should-i-have.

Qu, L., Knight, K., & Higgins, D. (2016, September). Same-sex couple families in Australia. Retrieved from https://aifs.gov.au/publications/same-sex-couple-families-australia.

Thorpe, J. R. (2017, May 12). Here's how women fought for the right to be educated. Retrieved from https://www.bustle.com/p/heres-how-women-fought-for-the-right-to-be-educated-throughout-history-53150.

Women in Super (2021). The facts about women and super. Retrieved from https://www.womeninsuper.com.au/content/the-facts-about-women-and-super/gjumzs.

# 2 Contemporary women, can we even have it all?

No need to hurry. No need to sparkle. No need to be anybody but oneself.
—Virginia Woolf (1929)

Female immigrants [to Australia during the convict period] were subjected to the same kind of treatment as the women convicts. Whenever news spread that a shipload of female immigrants was due to arrive, hordes of men would assemble at the docks, waiting to claim their share of the 'imported goods'. These women had to wait six-and-a-half hours before being given any food and their sleeping arrangements consisted of

> a few dozen blankets (for nearly 100 women) and as many bed ticks, in which the girls were set to put straw, so that they might have something better than the bare boards to lie down upon. By contrast, the 320 convicts who had landed that same morning had been immediately provided with clothing and rations. The Governor had welcomed them and they were given sleeping berths ... The fate of women was one of exploitation and abuse.
>
> (Anne Summers, 1994, pp. 323–324)

## A room of one's own

You probably well know the story of Virginia Woolf who was asked in the late 1920s to give a couple of lectures to the women's colleges at the University of Cambridge. They were compiled into Woolf's famous essay, A Room of One's Own. In it, she expounded on the theme of women in fiction. She wrote that a woman must have money and a room of her own if she is to write (Woolf, 1929). Many since have taken that word 'fiction' to stand in for other things. As academics, we take it as a stand in for non-fiction writing, journal articles, an academic career including simply preparing lessons for our students. As we write here today, we are all simultaneously doing hundreds of different things as diverse as stopping the dog from barking as the mail arrives to making sandwiches for children.

DOI: 10.4324/9781003020554-3

We are nagging children to do their music practice, once they have eaten their sandwiches of course (nothing wrecks a piano more than jammy hands), emailing colleagues, chasing up PhD students who have been on leave and trying to drink a coffee which is cold. How many of us actually get a hot cup of coffee?

But, as Woolf rightly points out, it was only very recently that women no longer had to endure, what Woolf described as, being "denied the right to possess what money they earned", instead, every dollar women of the past earned was "taken from [them] and disposed of according to [their] husband's [or their father's] wisdom" so what was his, was his and what was hers was also his. Women were as much a possession as their husband's furniture and house.

Of course, we have come a long way. We are now allowed to not only keep our own money but to earn it. We do not have to stop working just because we are married or pregnant or a mum. We do not have to give our money to our father and then to our husband who owns not only everything we do but us and our children as well. Long story short, we have come a long way baby. But, we still have a long way to go. When the COVID-19 pandemic sent many people, globally, to work from home, it was women who still took the lion's share of the household work in many households around the world, despite juggling everything else they had to do in a normal workday. Besides that, the workplace is not exactly easy for women or fair or even equal. We might have the right to work, but do we enjoy the right to as many promotions as our male counterparts? Do we enjoy the same luxuries of just being ourselves as them? Can we say no? Can we lift ourselves out of the expectation to be perfect all the time? I wonder if the privilege of being male, male privilege we have been told all about, is actually the privilege of not needing to excuse themselves, of not needing to explain themselves and of not needing a sticker that said "boys can do anything" because that was just a given. Perhaps, being a girl meant having to justify your choices, and having to be made aware of those choices, while being a boy meant just knowing the world was your oyster. Is that male privilege? Maybe that male privilege we have been told about our whole lives, the kinds of privilege our male peers spoke of at school when they noted they did not have stupid stickers that said, "boys can do anything" because it was a given, hasn't changed that much.

It is not just the practical of the money and possessions, it is also the right to tell our own stories. As the medical research community has increasingly revealed (Burrows, 2021), it was not until the 1990s that medical testing included women's bodies, women are not fully human in the sense that we are not always allowed to be part of the story. Woolf talked about how much of the story of women was not written by us, instead, most books about women was written by men. And many of those books did not paint a nice picture. We were seen as inferior, as less than men. We can see it in other areas of our lives too, in our depiction as the 'weaker sex', in our 'emotional natures', in our lack of strength. We see even in psychology where Freud was fond of talking about phallus and lack, as if we did not have a penis and, instead, felt we were always lacking. Maybe, and this was Woolf's point, this obsession with women's weakness is not due to women, it is due to men. As if men need women to be inferior to maintain their existence. As if we women owe them their superiority so they can shoulder the burdens of life, and that burden is only shouldered by the self-confidence required to get up every day and do it all over again. As Woolf (1929, p. 30) again states:

> And how can we generate this imponderable quality, which is yet so invaluable, most quickly? By thinking that other people are inferior to oneself. By feeling that one has some innate superiority – it may be wealth, or rank, a straight nose, or the portrait of a grandfather by Romney – for there is no end to the pathetic devices of the human imagination – over other people. Hence the enormous importance to a patriarch who has to conquer, who has to rule, of feeling that great numbers of people, half the human race indeed, are by nature inferior to himself. It must indeed be one of the chief sources of his power.

And that was what she was railing against. She did not like, and we would say it is ridiculous, the idea that women are somehow inferior to men. That we are the weaker sex. That we are more likely to be 'good', whatever that means, at 'caring' and 'soft skill'. The back handed compliments of being told robots would not replace us because we have the skills required to meet the twenty-first century demands of being able to talk nicely to another human soul. That the skills that incline women towards becoming a teacher or a nurse or a child-carer were also the ones that would protect us from the robotisation of our work.

However, they are also dangerous. As the Gender Policy Report (Franceschet, Poscopo & Ruzycki, 2021) reveals, vaccine scepticism rates are much higher in women than in men, and it is women of childbearing age that remains the most sceptical about vaccines. This report was looking at COVID-19 vaccine but it is not an unusual position as women are more likely to be distrustful of medical intervention than men. Some suggest it is because women frequently report not being taken seriously, their pain and their health needs being minimised (Pagán, 2018). In addition, we lack the ability to tell our own stories about our health, and be believed by doctors (Jackson, 2019), that make women more likely to be distrustful of doctors' advice. Why bother telling our health stories when they are unlikely to be believed, as the stories of women being told they are hysterical when they have complex conditions like endo or fibro or any number of other health conditions. Endometriosis organisations, such as endometriosis.org, often report many myths about the condition that are not just prevalent in the wider community, they are frequently held by doctors too. Other hidden conditions, frequently experienced by women such as Lupus (Sloan et al., 2020) and fibromyalgia (sometimes called fibro) (Baxter, 2011) are frequently derided, misunderstood, thought to be 'just in a woman's head', and doctors are not always able to properly diagnose and understand the conditions. Combine these with issues raised in the media about police mishandling domestic violence situations (McKenzie & Tozer, 2020) and the low rates of reporting of sexual assault, data suggest around half of women who are assaulted don't report or seek advice about it because they fear they won't be believed (Australian Institute of Health and Welfare – AIHW, 2020), and you have women feeling like they are not going to be believed whatever they say and a lack of trust in authorities and in establishment methods of correcting disorders. Even without the violence that is perpetrated on women's bodies, do we still think it a fit and proper question to ask, "can women have it all?". It is sexist to ask that question; one we never ask men.

Despite having the ability to work and earn our own money we are still under enormous pressure to conform. We are expected to be superwoman, to have it all, to be it all at work and at home, all the time being awesome and perfect and amazing and polite. We are also encouraged to be under enormous pressure; to be busy is to be important to be something. However, in this chapter, we want to ask if that is actually the way we should go. After all, and quoting from Woolf again, she knew that all we needed was enough money and a room of one's own if we were to do anything. She talks of her aunt who died and left her a stipend on which she could rely for the rest of her life

> No force in the world can take from me... Food, house and clothing are mine forever. Therefore, not merely do effort and labour cease, but also hatred and bitterness. I need not hate any man; he cannot hurt me. I need not flatter any man; he has nothing to give me.

## How are women represented in the media?

When you think of how women are represented in the media, it is Anne Summers book of 1975, *Damned Whores and God's Police* that is immediately instructive. In that book, Summers described how then (perhaps still?) women were described as having a certain hair colour, or whether they were married, or not, and their hair colour before their occupation or their achievement was outlined. As a report from Cardiff outlined (Kitzinger, Chimba, Williams, Haran & Boyce, 2008), it is not unusual to read of a woman who achieved something, anything, and, later down the piece, also learn that she is blonde, when she was born, the number of children she is borne and her marital status.

Women politicians are the same, Julia Gillard was pilloried by those in opposition to her because she did not have any children. Women who do not follow a traditional path, who do not marry, who do not have children, frequently experience this kind of criticism. And, the criticism can be fairly benign – "when are you going to have children?" or "oh, you will be sorry if you do not have children" to the quite awful, "it is a women's job to have children". Sometimes this message is obvious, some random at the bus stop asks you if you have any kids and if not, why. However, media messaging around women who are politicians and women celebrities, look at how they are judged for everything from how they look to how they grieve shows women that their job is still to be a mother, that is their primary role and their primary joy comes from having children.

Women are increasingly choosing not to have children. The total fertility rate in Australia is illustrated in Figure 2.1, graph taken from Families in Australia Survey published by the Institute of Family Studies (2015). See Figure 2.1 below.

That one of the authors of this book has five kids, and another three, makes them quite unusual as those rates are more like the 1960s than the 2020s! In 2017, the Australian Bureau of Statistics was reporting childless couples was likely to be the most common family type in Australia in the next decade (Corsetti, 2017). Australian National University (ANU, 2017) data suggest that around 17% of women, or almost one in five, in the 40–44 age group, so women at the end of their reproductive lives, are childless. This statistic is averaged with education massively impacting on childlessness. The same report found that approximately 30% of women with a postgraduate degree were childless, compared with 19% with a bachelor's degree and 17% who have completed year 12. Location seems to also impact with women living in remote areas having, on average, one extra child compared to women in the cities.

# Total fertility rate

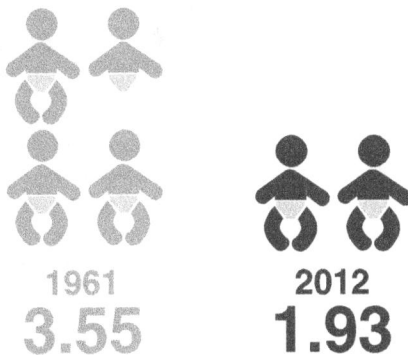

1961
3.55

2012
1.93

*Figure 2.1* Fertility rate in Australia.
Source: Australian Institute of Family Studies (2015).

For many women, this choice is economic. It is about their bodies but it is also about not being able to meet the high bar set for mothers. Mothers are seen to be judged more harshly than any other group, and that judgement often comes from nearest and dearest (Klass, 2017). Single mothers are seen less positively than single fathers (Brown, 2019), and they also judge themselves more harshly (June, 2016). The reasons increasing numbers of women reject motherhood are complex and range from choosing to opt out of a primary site of oppression (Ireland, 1993), to a lack of opportunities and options, or not finding a father 'in time' (Morell, 1994). For others (Snitow, 1992), it was feminism's inability to critique motherhood without putting it down that was an issue.

## What does it mean to be a superwoman?

If we go back to Woolf, in her essay she mentions the idea of a sister for Shakespeare. The thought experiment is as much about theorising what would have happened if a woman, of equal talent and birth to Shakespeare, had tried to be a writer, a poet, in the 1600s. Shakespeare did have a sister but there is no evidence she was a poet or even a writer. But, Woolf wants us to wonder what would have happened to her, would she have had his success? She says no, because she would likely have "died young – alas she never wrote a word". But she stands in for all the women who have never had the opportunities we have had, the ones where we have been educated, and seen as just as deserving of an education as a male, as our brothers or, at least I hope you have had that experience. She says we have to think of this poor woman, who died and never wrote a word, because she lives in all of us, but she is never heard. Woolf calls out to all the women "who are not here tonight, for they are washing up the dishes and putting the children to bed". Woolf wanted us to know that that poet lives in all of us, if we give them the opportunity to live and to breath. But it is hard. It is hard because putting the children to bed, washing the dishes and keeping on top of the laundry, which frequently falls to women, is hard and it saps your time and your energy and it's easier to just do that. It is easier to not be, to put children to bed and to wash dishes, than it is to be something. But, is it enough to be something?

We are now under pressure to be everything, girls can do anything, all the time. We are given the opportunities our grandmothers and great grandmothers were denied. But at what cost? And, is it enough to be a woman who does anything or do we have to do everything? If we do everything, we will need superpowers. We will need to be superwomen. But, is that what we all want? And at what cost?

When you look at the ways that women present themselves on all the social media sites, it all looks so awesome. I am sure we all have that friend, that cousin, that old high-school acquaintance who is busy on the socials making her life appear super glamourous and awesome and fun and exciting and perfect. It could be those women living in a fabulous beach location with their linen tunics, their perfectly shiny hair, their children with long, but not too long, hair and their perfect white teeth. Or it could be your friend from your kid's school who bakes bread every Saturday from the sourdough starter she got from her grandmother (hashtag baking). Or, that mother who is on a yoga retreat (hashtag health is happiness). Or that botoxed friend with the perfect smile who does craft with her kids on school holidays, making Christmas decorations from air-dry clay and paint without wrecking her clothes, the kids' clothes or the house (hashtag memories for life). Or the woman who travels regularly with her amazing husband. But, it is on a deeper, less privileged level too. It is the inability to admit this gig of being a mum and a person who has a job is hard. Let alone keeping a career going when there are little kids at home. It is hard when you are up all night with a kid who is teething/spewing/pooping/crying and you have to drag yourself out of bed and make a coffee and front up at the office the next day and be coherent. Is that the superwoman? Is that Shakespeare's sister?

## The pressures on women to have it all

Have you ever had that experience where you really wanted to say, 'no', but didn't? Maybe you felt you could not? Maybe you felt you should not? Many women have had the experience of saying yes and being uncomfortable because the alternative might have been much more dangerous. Maybe it is a work thing, and you feel conflicted about doing something that, on the one hand, had you really do not want to do, but, on the other, fear it may be the last opportunity that will come your way. Research suggests women are socialised (Lively, 2013) into saying yes. We tend to say yes because we are worried people might be sad, or mad, if we say no. We tend to say yes because we are taught to be 'more in touch with our feelings' and, this one is especially true on the dating market, to be liked and to tie that feeling of being liked to our self-worth, our niceness and our ability to be empathetic to others' feelings. This stuff is all fine, it is nice to not want to be mean to others. But, it often comes at a cost to our own feelings, our sense of agency and our time. The latter is the only commodity we get given and cannot get more of. This point is not only for dating or for friendships or for the random on the street asking us to change our electricity supplier, it is also at work. Women, studies show, are less likely to say no at work than men. And, maybe that is because, "we will be seen as helpful", "we will get ahead because we are keen", "the boss will love us, they will think we are an awesome team player" or something else. Actually, the research says that is not true. We do not come across as helpful, if that even is an end goal. We do not come across as keen, we do not even come across as a team player. Research

(Gross, 2016) suggests that far from making us look like we are able to think in large swathes about our organisation, or clients or our world, we just look dependable. Far from being the Arabian horse we desire to be seen, we look like the Clydesdale who is unwavering, yes, a hard worker, absolutely, but not really promotion material. We lack that wow factor, that je-ne-sais-quoi of the Arabian horse.

It comes back to socialisation, women are socialised to be people pleasers (Scheer & Prakash, 2019). To say yes is to not have to confront the hard questions of how do we say no in a respectful and honest way (Gross, 2016). It also leads to us working ourselves to death without the rewards and the accolades men take for granted. Frequently, our willingness to do the grunt work, the unattractive work, the work that does not garner the praise and the accolades leads us to give to men the power over us and to give away, like the things that we were denied in our grandmother's day before we could possess property, our humanity. One of the ways we get that power back is with one, monosyllabic word, "no". If you need to practice, because research (Jennings-Edquist, 2020) suggests most women actually do, take a few moments to say no to your reflection in the mirror. It helps to see what you look like when you say no and to consider how saying no actually won't break your face or cause anything else to happen.

Saying no is important because it allows you to take back some power. You do not need to be mean about it, you do not need to spit the word at your boss or your friend who calls you at midnight to tell you about her latest drama. But, it is an important word. Start with little things. If you are asked to work on something that is outside of the requirements of your job, and will probably take time away from you doing the core business of your role, you can say no. There, we are giving you that permission.

It is also important to say no so you do not waste the most valuable resource you have, your time. If we say no, that we have enough, that maybe the boss can ask another employee to do it, to seek out another person whose workload is not as full as ours, or even that we are fine with our current electricity provider and we are really just at the shops to get some lunch, you are really saying "no, you do not have a right to all of my time, to my attention, to my stress levels". And, that is okay!

Why call things out with a no? Why don't men seem to have to say no? Because, research (Pham, 2016) says, there is an inherent bias in the workplace that sees women as more compliant, as easier to manipulate and to get to do the basic bitch work of the office. Women need to be responsibilised to say no, because men do not have to say no, nobody is wasting their time with the same petty tasks as they are wasting women's time with. Even if you are on the same level as your male counterparts, who cleans up the UberEats after the late night meeting? At home, and sadly this has not changed much since Woolf's day, who is doing the dishes? Who is putting the kids to bed?

**BOX 2.1  DANI AND SAYING NO**

Dani is a year 4 teacher at a large suburban primary school. Her school is a prep to 12 school in the inner suburbs of a large city. The school has about 1500 students, and there are 800 in the primary school. Her cohort is diverse, with many special education needs, a high refugee and migrant population and a transitory population so she's always got newcomers but equally, a large population leave, sometimes they just disappear. That means she's always got to chase up where the students have gone and try to follow them up on the department's system. She is also a single mum of four children, two attend her primary school, one is in the high school and one is finished school.

If you are exhausted reading that story, we were too. We asked Dani how she manages.

"I am a perfectionist," Dani told us. "So, I put a lot of pressure on myself. A few years ago, when my oldest was about to finish grade 12, I realised I was taking on too much. Back then, I was also the DP, Deputy Principal. I had a tonne of responsibilities, I was the deputy in charge of curriculum, so I had standardised testing, interim testing to see how kids were progressing in non-standardised testing years (the students are assessed in primary school at years 3 and 5) and also intake testing. We also do leave testing, both of the kids' academic achievement and social achievement. We also interview the parents. All that was my job. I also was in charge of supply teaching, so I had to be at work at 6.30am every school day to field the calls of sick teachers and try to find replacements. Our school had 800 kids and that meant usually trying to find a replacement for 10 teachers a day. It was hectic.

I always put such pressure on myself, always have since I was a kid. When our [standardised test] scores dopped, I blamed myself. What should I have done differently to help them do better? How will people see me at the school? In the department?

"And, yeah, the department. They put so much pressure on schools to achieve. Our school had special funding, thankfully that was the school manager's (what used to be called the bursar) responsibility and the principal but I had to spend some of it on curriculum development and enrichment. So, I was under huge amounts of pressure to choose the right programs, to have the teachers be satisfied and the students' grades improve.

"But, trying to juggle all that responsibility on top of my son's year 12 was too much. I wound up nearly having a breakdown and talked extensively to my doctor who asked me who I was doing all this for? Helping my son was my pleasure, and I really wanted to do that, but all the other stuff? For whom was I doing all that? Who benefited?

*(Continued)*

"Two pieces of advice really stuck with me. One was from a colleague, the other Deputy Principal who oversaw behaviour. She said, "Dani, there are loads of other people who can do the job, if you need to step back and take a break, you know what? The sun will still shine, the sky wont' fall in, I promise it'll be alright". Turns out she is pretty smart at managing people, she must be to be a DP who manages behaviour. The second piece of advice was from my doctor. He asked me who was getting the best of me and was that the best allocation of my limited resources".

"So, I decide I had nothing to lose by stepping back. When I was offered a chance to go on a four-day retreat to do some curriculum planning with other large schools in the state, I said no. Then, I started saying no to other stuff. I took my long service leave. I finally took it! And, you know what, the person who acted my job did great. So, when I came back I had a sit-down with my Principal. I said I wanted to go back into the classroom, that was why I became a teacher, to teach kids.

"I learned that people do not really notice if you say no. They just get on and find someone else. I do not know why I did not start taking a bit of a step back sooner. It sounds harsh to say, but there are other people who can do your job, it is okay to take a step back and say no. It is also okay to honour what you really want to do, in my case it's teach Year 4. That is not a standardised testing year, and it is a great one to teach, the kids are all older but not too old, and I love the curriculum, we do fractions in that year and it is great to make food and enjoy a really practical approach to teaching.

"Remember, we need a room of our own. Woolf told us that. Now we have an (open plan) office with a (hot?) desk, we have the same space as a man, but does that stop us being responsible to be everything to everyone all the time? Once again, the words of Virginia Woolf are weirdly prescient and instructive. She spoke about how small her stipend was, the 500 pound a year she was gifted on her aunt's death, but how it was a release, a release from the need to chase money. She questioned why "the stockbroker and the great barrister going indoors to make money and more money and more money when it is a fact that 500 pounds a year will keep one alive in the sunshine". For her, the importance of that money was that it was a release, a release to freedom which was, as she noted "freedom to think of things in themselves".

Her work is, in a way, a scream against the tyranny that pits one sex against another, that puts women down as inferior just because of their sex. It is also a scream against the modern world, against chasing down money and stuff for no good purpose. If you have enough, why do you need more? Do you really need to have it all? Maybe you just need to choose which bits of all you really want and just enjoy keeping yourself alive in the sunshine.

# Reference list

AIHW (2020, 28 August). Sexual assault in Australia. Retrieved from https://www.aihw.gov.au/getmedia/0375553f-0395-46cc-9574-d54c74fa601a/aihw-fdv-5.pdf.aspx?inline=true.

ANU (2017, June 27). Census 2016: Location and education affects how many children you have. Retrieved from https://www.anu.edu.au/news/all-news/census-2016-location-and-education-affects-how-many-children-you-have.

Australian Institute of Family Studies (AIFS, 2015, October 20). Australian family facts and figures released on World Statistic Day. Retrieved from https://aifs.gov.au/media-releases/australian-family-facts-and-figures-released-world-statistics-day.

Baxter, D. (2011). Fibromyalgia misconceptions: Interview with a Mayo Clinic expert. Retrieved from https://www.mymlc.com/health-information/articles/f/fibromyalgia-misconceptions-interview-with-a-mayo-clinic-expert/?section=What%20is%20the%20most%20common%20misconception%20about%20fibromyalgia?

Brown, M. (2015, November 25). Single moms vs single dads: Examining the double standards of single parenthood. Retrieved from (https://www.parents.com/parenting/dynamics/single-parenting/single-moms-vs-single-dads-a-look-at-the-double-standards-of-single-parenthood-how-we-can-do-better/.

Burrows, K. (2021, March 8). Gender bias in medicine and medical research is still putting women's health at risk. Retrieved from https://theconversation.com/gender-bias-in-medicine-and-medical-research-is-still-putting-womens-health-at-risk-156495.

Corsetti, S. (2017, May 15). Childless couples 'on track to be Australia's most common family type'. Retrieved from https://www.abc.net.au/news/2017-05-15/childless-households-on-the-rise/8528546.

Franceschet, S., Piscopo, J., & Ruzycki, S. (2021, January 19). To overcome women's vaccine scepticism, take its roots seriously. Retrieved from https://genderpolicyreport.umn.edu/to-overcome-womens-vaccine-skepticism-take-its-roots-seriously/.

Gross, E. (2016, September 19). When to say 'no' at work (and why it's important). Retrieved from https://www.forbes.com/sites/elanagross/2016/09/19/when-to-say-no-at-work/?sh=3ad8c0be1322.

Ireland, M. S. (1993). *Reconceiving women: Separating motherhood from female identity.* New York: Guilford Press.

Jackson, G. (2019, September 2). Why don't doctors trust women? Because they don't know much about us. Retrieved from https://www.theguardian.com/books/2019/sep/02/why-dont-doctors-trust-women-because-they-dont-know-much-about-us.

Jennings-Edquist, G. (2020, November 18). How and when to say no at work. Retrieved from https://www.abc.net.au/everyday/how-to-say-no-at-work/12821000.

June, L. (2016, June 17). Mothers feel more judged than fathers. Retrieved from https://www.thecut.com/2016/06/mothers-feel-more-judged-than-fathers.html.

Kitzinger, J., Chimba, M. D., Williams, A., Haran, J., & Boyce, T. (2008). Gender, stereotypes and expertise in the press: How newspapers represent female and male scientists. UK Resource Centre for Women in Science, Engineering and Technology (UKRC) and Cardiff University. Retrieved from https://orca.cardiff.ac.uk/28633/1/Kitzinger_Report_2.pdf

Klass, P. (2017, August 7). Most mothers feel judged with families often the worst critics. Retrieved from https://www.nytimes.com/2017/08/07/well/family/most-mothers-feel-judged-with-families-often-the-worst-critics.html.

Lively, K. (2013, November 2). Why women have a hard time saying no. Retrieved from https://www.psychologytoday.com/au/blog/smart-relationships/201311/ why-women-have-hard-time-saying-no.

McKenzie, N., & Tozer, J. (2020, December 6). 'Hidden crisis': When your domestic abuser is also the local police officer. Retrieved from https://www.smh.com. au/national/hidden-crisis-when-your-domestic-abuser-is-also-the-local-police-officer-20201203-p56k6r.html.

Morell, C. M. (1994). *Unwomanly conduct: The challenges of intentional childlessness.* New York: Psychology Press.

Pagán, C. (2018, May 3). When doctors downplay women's health concerns. Retrieved from https://www.nytimes.com/2018/05/03/well/live/when-doctors-downplay-womens-health-concerns.html.

Pham, T. (2016, December 20). Think you're not biased against women at work? Read this. Retrieved from https://www.forbes.com/sites/break-the-future/2016/12/20/ think-youre-not-biased-against-women-at-work-read-this/?sh=77ef71dc7e5a.

Scheer, A., & Prakash, V. (2019). Advancing women's rights from within: The story of the alliance for women in medicine and science. In M.T. Segal., K. Kelly., & V. Demos (Eds.), *Gender and Practice: Knowledge, Policy, Organizations* (pp. 163– 180). Bingley, UK: Emerald Publishing Limited.

Sloan, M., Naughton, F., Harwood, R., Lever, E., D'Cruz, D., Sutton, S., Walia, C., Howard, P., & Gordon, C. (2020). Is it me? The impact of patient–physician interactions on lupus patients' psychological well-being, cognition and health-care-seeking behavior. *Rheumatology Advances in Practice, 4*(2), rkaa037. doi:10.1093/ rap/rkaa037.

Snitow, A. (1992). Feminism and motherhood: An American reading. *Feminist Review, 40*(1), 32–51.

Summers, A. (1994). *Damned whores and god's police.* Melbourne, Australia: New-South Publishing.

Woolf, V. (1929). *A room of one's own.* New York: Harcourt, Brace and Company.

# 3 The changing nature of work and the impact on women

> If you don't think about and plan for the future of work, then your organisation has no future.
>
> —Jacob Morgan

## The future of work

Back when we were kids, we pictured a future that somewhat resembled the opening song of 'The Jetsons' – robots and machinery made life easier for the Jetsons, from making breakfast, through the commute to work, and tasks undertaken at work. Of course, the future has not unfolded exactly like that, but there is no denying the increasing impact of technology on our daily lives, from Siri telling you about the weather for the day ahead, to Google Home playing your favourite music mix, or simply being able to ask your car to make a phone call during your commute to work. We have jewellery that can tell women when their period is due, or how well they're sleeping, and wearable apps that tell people to move more, stress less, or take a deep breath. The COVID-19 pandemic, resulting in workplaces globally moving employees to working from home, almost overnight, would have been a lot less manageable without Zoom, Skype, Teams, Facetime, or other virtual communication devices. There is no denying we are becoming increasingly comfortable with technology impacting on every facet of our lives. Despite all of this, how ready are we for the 'future of work?'

In 2013, academics Frey and Osborne indicated that almost 50% of jobs would be made obsolete in near future, due to computerisation. While the future of work is increasingly being discussed in the media, and in academic research and books, interventions to address it are less frequently considered. The role of gender in all of this also lacks attention.

Consultants from EY Australia, Andrews and Friday (2019) say that we need to "stop talking about the future of work!" If that sounds crazy, you need to understand – they aren't saying it isn't imperative, they're saying "workplace disruption is (already) here. So why aren't we acting on it?"

DOI: 10.4324/9781003020554-4

Talking, in other words, simply isn't enough. We need those interventions. We need to be addressing it. Additionally, Emma Hogan, the NSW Public Service Commissioner, stated:

> I think it is really important that the discussion about 'work of the future', which technically could be renamed 'work of the now', isn't all doom and gloom. We should view this as an opportunity to introduce and co-design change that benefits people and communities.

We, the authors of this book, agree. This is an opportunity, but it's something about which we need to be proactive. Being reactive, on the other hand, will not be enough.

Under a gender lens, the research all suggests that, while there are opportunities for women, women, collectively, could be left behind if they don't leap into the opportunities. Taking advantages of these opportunities could result in more productive and better paid roles, but if women don't take action, the gender disparity in terms of leadership roles and pay gaps can only increase (Madgavkar et al., 2019). To adapt to new ways of working, women need to be more skilled, mobile, and tech savvy than ever before (Madgavkar et al., 2019). In other words, the future of work cannot be ignored, and especially by women who need to be certain they are not left behind in the business of the future. This chapter ponders the changing nature of work, the impact of this on women, and women upskilling for the future of work.

## The changing workplace

The changing nature of work is an issue that cannot be ignored by women. Data suggests that the impact on women will fall predominately in lower paying occupations, such as clerical services. It is expected that between 2017 and 2030, there will be a decline in women in these roles in mature economies. Currently, 17% of women are in clerical roles, but this is expected to decline to 14% of women in mature economies by 2030 (Madgavkar et al., 2019).

It is anticipated that men would still outnumber women in the highest paying roles – managers, legislators, and senior officials (Madgavkar et al., 2019). Women often put their careers on hold to have babies, or for other caring responsibilities (beyond children). Some women are included in the 'Sandwich Generation' where they end up having children later in life and find themselves caring for small children and ageing parents at the same time. Career interruptions, such as caring responsibilities, can result in women having bigger career gaps, and gaps in understanding the changed technology. Even working part time can result in less understanding of rapidly changing technologies, and frequently negatively impacts on career progression.

Jobs that are deemed 'women's jobs' are more likely to be impacted by partial automation, rather than full automation. As we discussed briefly in the last chapter, women are slightly less at risk of being displaced by technology automation than men are, because certain industries are more impacted than others. The gig economy relies on digital work platforms, and these are growing fastest in service roles, including food service, tourism, and retail where females often dominate (Madgavkar et al., 2019), however again, these industries are more likely to be impacted by partial automation, rather than full automation. Women are also more likely to be in roles such as clerical support, where routine cognitive tasks could be automated (Madgavkar et al., 2019), but, as we said before, the soft skills, those humanised and caring aspects of the role will still be required. Agriculture and driving are mostly likely to be affected, and apparently driving is one of the top professions for many men, globally. The gender divide and impact of automation is also worse in some countries (e.g., India) compared to others (Madgavkar et al., 2019). This difference is because of the dominance of roles at risk of becoming fully automated – physical roles such as machine operators.

## The gig economy

Ah, the gig economy. It sounds exciting and vibrant, doesn't it? Sometimes it is. Sometimes it's a choice. On the other hand, sometimes it is the only option to make ends meet or get a foot in the door of a particular industry. The gig economy is "a labour market characterised by the prevalence of short-term contracts or freelance work as opposed to permanent jobs" (Oxford Advanced Learner Dictionary, 2020). While a lot of the research suggests that Millennials and other young people are 'opting' for the flexibility the gig economy provides, 'opting' may imply more agency than is really there. Some industries, such as writing and editing, have traditionally been structured around a 'gig' approach, not really giving people a choice. Others, including academia, tend to rely on a lot of part time staff to support their workplace structure.

All that said, the gig economy must be great for women, right? Women really want flexibility, don't they? Apparently not always, even though that is what we are frequently told. A survey of 2109 Australian women under 40 found that 80% of women want a secure job, while 62% of respondents wanted flexibility (Baird et al., 2018). Also, women working casually or on a freelance basis were also more likely to feel that they did not have the opportunity to progress into senior roles compared with those working full time (Baird et al., 2018). Ninety-six percent of women want job security, but just 59% of women report they have job security (Baird et al., 2018). Furthermore, over a quarter of women (28%) worry about their role becoming automated, or that they might lose their job due to automation. This is a universal concern, however, and more males worry about this than women (Baird et al., 2018).

Women have indicated that it can be challenging to juggle carer responsibilities with the 'gigs' in their gig economy career. Perhaps this juggle is why 61% of women in the gig economy in the USA would like to make their gig a full-time role, rather than relying on gigs (Hyperwallet, 2017). This desire has been reported to sometimes result in women opting to leave children at home while doing a quick job, or some women being left behind others on the platform who get rated higher due to their more regular availability (Hunt & Samman, 2019). Also, due to the unstable nature of 'gigs', and how these roles can be quickly impacted with economic changes, or changing organisational or societal priorities, it is important to address ways to protect these workers from precarious working conditions. Calls for changes to Government policies and organisational processes have been made to work towards enabling a fairer and more stable income (Hunt & Samman, 2019).

Women tend to do a variety of freelance or 'gig' roles, from professional services (e.g., Writing), direct selling (usually through multilevel marketing), or service platforms and organisations (such as task-based sites and services like food delivery). Interestingly, according to a US study, 88% of female workers in the gig economy have completed at least some University study, if not an entire degree (Hyperwallet, 2017).

---

**BOX 3.1  MICHELLE AND JUGGLING IT ALL**

Midwife, Michelle, works technically 'part time' at 0.7. She doesn't have children, but lives with her primary partner, and is in a polyamorous relationship. Michelle knew she was polyamorous since she was young, and she said that "disrupted the idea of marriage very early on while I was still a late teen verging into adulthood. I always thought I'd have children and in the last couple of years have put to rest and processed that I wouldn't be having my own child".

We asked Michelle how she juggles it all.

> I'm a frontline health worker – a midwife. I put an immense amount of pressure on myself for work because it's dealing with people's lives and wellbeing. It's crucial, challenging work and I love it. But nothing in me will allow me to take it for granted. I measure my success by how those I am caring for feel about how they're transitioning to parenthood, how their feeding is improving, how they feel about the support they are receiving and how they feel they're recovering. I am more relaxed around household responsibilities.

She explained that the household work is,

> mostly on me, but when I'm struggling or in the middle of a heavy shift rotation, he will take more of it on – he tries to take it on more

equally but struggles, it's a work in progress. He takes on several aspects of things that I don't have to think about, but they're not necessarily everyday things, like cooking/meal planning and so on. We try to divide things but it is imperfect. I track and manage things in my head more, but we've similar levels of cleanliness and motivation. My 'training' from childhood on how to do things was better. We have discussions at semi-regular intervals as part of continually trying to equalise things – especially given the nature of society, patriarchy and shift work.

She said "to feel like I've recharged, days off are important". She explained "I love reading, I love podcasts, tv, movies, video games. I also love cooking and when I can relax or feel inspired it's more a hobby and enjoyable than a chore".

When we asked how she juggles it all, she said,

Hypervigilance. This is not a tip, it is a coping mechanism, it has the benefits, but also significant draw backs so I don't recommend it. I suspect it is pretty common though. What I mean by it is tracking everything constantly so that tiny changes can be made at any moment as needed to minimise the need for big changes, or big shifts that cause issues, I never stop noticing what's going on around me, what might need to happen, what's coming up, what just passed that might need follow up, and also to a fairly significant degree, where my partner is at too.

She also gave practical suggestions:

practical things I use are Habitica, my calendar, Trello and my idiosyncratic means of triaging email across my various accounts. There are deep holes of links saved to go back to in several places that I doubt I'll ever get to, but I know where they are should there be five minutes spare. I prioritise sleep, which sounds weird as a time management technique but all things work better with enough sleep and as a shift worker I'm deeply present to this, so I will sometimes prioritise sleep over other practical things if I can manage it because I know it will help the other things anyway.

## Implications for women

The rapid changes in work have resulted in disruption and change for all workers. Research shows that workers must develop in demand skills as well as the flexibility and mobility needed to negotiate labour market transitions. Workers will also need the appropriate knowledge and access to technology and ability to be involved in the creation of technology. The challenge for women is how to juggle these changes, particularly because social and structural barriers faced by women in organisations can be particularly problematic in ensuring women adapt to the changed workforce. Technology and innovation can result in more gender equality in the workforce, but women can be supported by leaders in the public and private sectors to foster this equality and ensure women have appropriate skills (Madgavkar et al., 2019).

The gender gap is not based on education. Women in mature economies graduate from higher education at rates equal to, or even higher than, men. The concern is that women don't study in high-growth fields, resulting in professional, scientific, and technical roles (Madgavkar et al., 2019). In developing economies, there are still large gaps in education between males and females, and in emerging economies, women are increasingly positioned to be prepared for the changing workforce, due to increased education for females.

Just 20% of tech workers are females in mature economies and only 1.4% of female workers work in the development, maintenance, or operation of ICT systems, compared with 5.5% of male workers in OECD counties (Madgavkar et al., 2019). In developing countries, the gender divide persists, as would be expected, but globally, men are 33% more likely to have internet access than women, and women tend to be less likely to enrol in STEM degrees, particularly information and communication technology. Globally, women represent just 35% of total STEM students, but most of these are enrolled in science degrees (Madgavkar et al., 2019).

Lifelong learning, from school to employment, and throughout their working lives, needs to be addressed by women. Women are encouraged to take advantage of training and reskilling through academic institutions, or within their organisations or industry bodies. Studies have shown that showing that organisations are more likely to offer training and support for staff (Madgavkar et al., 2019). In 2014, just 20% of organisations reported offering this, but by 2018, 54% of organisations were reporting offering training and development opportunities (Madgavkar et al., 2019), and this is a trend we foresee will continue to rise with the increasing demands of the contemporary workplace. Reskilling is something governmental officers are increasingly considering for various governmental policies.

## Skills we need to develop

To support women in the changing nature of work, it is recommended that we consider ways to integrate women and build skills. As Sheryl Sandberg stated previously, "Women need to shift from thinking 'I'm not ready to do that' to thinking 'I want to do that- and I'll learn by doing it'".

McKinsey and Company makes a number of recommendations for the Government, private sector, and non-Government organisations to get involved in. We have analysed the research, and suggest the following for organisations seeking to increase opportunities and skilling for women:

Training and reskilling

- Training and apprenticeship programs for women
- Reskilling opportunities for women returning to the workforce
- Subsidise transition costs
- Government or Corporate reskilling subsidies for targeted occupations/ sectors
- Provide childcare subsidies for parents undergoing reskilling or pursuing higher education
- Invest in digital platforms
- The private sector and NGOs can develop free MOOCs
- Increase transparency on labour demand trends
- Technical school or university curriculums should be co-created with industry
- Organisations should develop information campaigns targeting women

Key actors can also help women to address labour mobility constraints, such as balancing paid and unpaid work. This could be through providing more accessible childcare and having corporate policies that provide flexible work options, or options enabling women to work at home. Providing more dynamic career paths and networks for women are important. This can be done through mentoring arrangements, sponsoring network building organisations for women, offering implicit bias training, and emphasising this in performance reviews and recruitment, and supporting women to find opportunities. Reducing stereotypes around gendered occupations are also important and can be done by increasing the public visibility of female role models in male dominated career areas. It should be noted, however, that women in male dominated areas are frequently required to speak on panels at conferences, in the media, etc., which can result in an output divide between males and females.

Finally, increasing women's representation in technology is important. One way to do this is to create pathways for women in STEM. This can be done from primary school to university, through providing internships, mentoring programs and apprenticeships, and sponsoring women perusing advanced education in STEM. STEM and STEM professions are ones that highlight the importance of lifelong learning (LLL). Studies (see, for example, Jaeger, Hudson, Pasque & Ampaw, 2017) argue that LLL has a massive impact on women's careers, outside of their career interruptions and decisions. Other studies (Rahim, Mohamed, Amrin & Mohammad, 2019) have argued it can help women navigate and negotiate their careers in STEM and other science and mathematically based careers and adapt to the dynamic and changing nature of their work. In all cases, it is choosing the right kinds of courses, ones that align with women's career goals and align those goals with their industry that assist them in transitioning through the various stages of their careers.

Providing greater support for women to develop digital skills, through programs to target women such as initiatives around digital and mobile literacy are also important. The Government, and corporations, should also consider pathways for women in the gig economy, including greater worker protections. Finally, addressing the funding gap for female entrepreneurs is important, through mentoring, greater diversity within venture capital firms, and increased funding access for female entrepreneurs in emerging markets (Madgavkar et al., 2019).

One of our authors works part time. We always joke among us that working part time in academia is just about doing a full-time role for part-time pay, because there is no real end point. Perhaps this is the same for all knowledge-based roles, and all roles where you can work from home. The to do list is never complete. In academia – there are always more papers to write, more essays to grade, more grants to apply for. We asked Rebecca to explain her part time, knowledge-based roles, and her reason for doing this. See Box 3.2 below.

---

**BOX 3.2  REBECCA'S PART TIME ROLE**

"I went back part time when I had my first child. I had been told I wouldn't be able to get pregnant, so naturally conceiving and having a baby at 34 was supposed to be a miracle. I really wanted to enjoy this time with my daughter, and to undo a lot of the problems from my own childhood, learn new patterns, new behaviours and new ways of being. As it turned out, I was able to have two more children, so I was very lucky. But, because of my research work, they are home educated, because they didn't want to go to school and knew from all the interviews they'd been privy too and my conversations in the media, that homeschool was a thing and it was possible and why would you go to school, get up every day to wear an outfit you don't want to do work you don't want to be trapped somewhere you don't want to be if you had a choice? I wouldn't either.

"Days are hectic. Sometimes, I'm waking up to coffee and then I'm homeschooling two kids (my youngest is still too young to do much, he just plays with some workbooks, or does some activities on his iPad) and do my work as well. When I have writing to do, the kids scarper and are nowhere to be seen. I am very lucky that I have a big yard and a lot of space. And, we have the means to pay someone to look after the kids when I am teaching. I'm also very lucky that my children are very helpful and attuned. There are other academic mothers in the homeschool community who talk about the benign neglect of the homeschooler, and how homeschooled children know their parents need space and are able to get on with their own lives while you get on with yours.

"But, it's hard graft. I don't get much downtime. I spend hours working on days I don't officially work to make up for all the things I have to get done. I take leave and then do work anyway.

Academic workloads are another issue. They don't necessarily reflect the effort or the hours required to do a task. If you have a student who's studying a research degree, they take up a lot of time, particularly around milestones. Then, there's the undergraduate cohorts who are in larger and larger classes and need more and more active management than they used to. There's less money about to buy marking support or teaching support. Grants are harder to come by and universities are on tight budgets.

"I find myself giving a lot of love and attention to my students, particularly my undergraduate cohorts, and having less for my own children during the busy times. There are also the endless committee assignments, marking, prep and the research expectation. I find myself writing on the weekends, at taekwondo, at music, at dancing, and at homeschool meetups (I'm very grateful to the other mums at homeschool groups who have my back, it really does take a village). Other things, like media interviews, aren't counted in workload but take up a lot of time. At least my children know what it's like behind the camera now and how unglamorous it really is being 'talent' on the TV news.

"Homeschooling, as many of us can remember from the COVID-19 school closures, takes a lot of time. I think my children are better at it than most because they do it all the time. But, there's still a reporting obligation and those can run to 40 pages ever ten months to maintain the legal right to homeschool. So, on top of doing my work, I'm also doing another job, that of a teacher. I'm a part-time academic, full-time mum, and full-time teacher.

"Coupling my many responsibilities with the few hours I have is tough. And to manage it, I have a lot of lists everywhere. I don't separate lists into different categories because, at the end of the day, it's all got to get done. I used to beat myself for not mopping the floor, we can't really afford a cleaner because I only work part time, but now I don't worry, because I'm only one person and we all take our shoes off at the door, that's as good as mopping, right?

"I'm also honest about what I can achieve. If I get very stressed and frazzled, and I yell at the kids, I carefully explain what's going on to them in an age-appropriate manner. I take responsibility and have some catchphrases I fall back on. "Count me, how many people am I?" is a favourite, and I know the children will joke about that in my eulogy. I also try to engage them with helping. They walk the dog when he needs to pee, they do the cat litter, they do the feeding of the pets. My son, who's eight, loves to do dishes.

"I'm also working hard on affirming to myself that I can only do what I can do. And that I'm happy to apologise for anything I do wrong. Another idiom I'm fond of is that it's better to beg forgiveness than ask permission. I'm learning how forgiving people are, and in spite of my inclination to try to do it all, to juggle everything, I have found a village who help me juggle".

## Where to from here?

This chapter, and the research which underpins it, might be a little overwhelming, or it could be seen as an exciting opportunity. The implications for all of us are that reskilling, refreshing training, and being aware of opportunities are important. The changing workplace impacts on both men and women, in many of the same ways, and also in some different ways. Women are generally more likely to be in a carer role, and where a couple has children, women tend to be more likely to be primary carers – this means that women may have more gaps in their experiences with organisation transitions and technology.

As a child, a Jetsons' world seemed rather exciting. The reality, as an adult, means that while it's exciting, we need to make it happen, and reachable for all!

## Reference list

Andrews, J., & Friday, C. (2019). Stop talking about the future of work. Retrieved from https://www.ey.com/en_au/future-of-work/stop-talking-about-the-future-of-work

Baird, M., et al. (2018). Women and the future of work. Retrieved from https://www.sydney.edu.au/content/dam/corporate/documents/business-school/research/women-work-leadership/women-and-the-future-of-work.pdf.

Frey, C., & Osborne, M. (2013). The future of employment: How susceptible are jobs to computerisation? *Oxford Martin*, 114. doi:10.1016/j.techfore.2016.08.019.

Hunt, A., & Samman, E. (2019). The flexible gig economy is not such a great option for women after all. Retrieved from https://www.opendemocracy.net/en/oureconomy/the-flexible-gig-economy-is-not-such-a-great-option-for-women-after-all/.

Hyperwallet (2017). The future of gig work is female. Retrieved from https://www.hyperwallet.com/app/uploads/HW_The_Future_of_Gig_Work_is_Female.pdf?mkt_tok=eyJpIjoiTVRjMU9UQmlOakk1TW1WaSIsInQiOiJYaVQrNEtTTzUzNWliUzZOSTQ3R2wxTnlwY00xZG9MZmErTnVXUkVJVdGhMRm9EUW9GWTFcL1huaXZPbnBmdGdN1R0BaWjAwa2tjTW5PXC82NnR5Z5Z0o1VFcrOFhWbEZMbVd3VUGcramZvdTg0Y1Y0Q3orMjljL1wvVUpJaFBBROVhMeXXRyU1QifQ%3D%3D.

Jaeger, A. J., Hudson, T. D., Pasque, P. A., & Ampaw, F. D. (2017). Understanding how lifelong learning shapes the career trajectories of women with STEM doctorates: The life experiences and role negotiations (LEARN) model. *The Review of Higher Education, 40*(4), 477–507.

Madgavkar, A., et al. (2019). The future of women at work: Transitions in the age of automation. Retrieved from https://www.mckinsey.com/featured-insights/gender-equality/the-future-of-women-at-work-transitions-in-the-age-of-automation#.

Oxford Advanced Learner's Dictionary (2020). Retrieved from https://www.oxfordlearnersdictionaries.com/definition/english/gig-economy

Rahim, A. N., Mohamed, Z. B., Amrin, A., & Mohammad, R. (2019, February). Women's dual roles and career growth: A preliminary study of Malaysian female talents in Science, Engineering and Technology (SET). *Journal of Physics: Conference Series, 1174*(1), 012013).

# 4  Ensuring well-being

It is not stress that kills us, it is our reaction to it.

—Hans Seyle

So far, we have discussed the historical roles of women in society, the changing nature of the workplace and the impact this has on women in the workplace. Given the changing nature of workplaces and the need for women to work in a variety of roles in such a fluid environment, we now turn to some of the challenges and pressure women faced in our lives. Many of us would agree that stress and being stressed out is something many of us experienced on a daily basis.

Stress is not a new concept. As far back as 1937, the British cardiologist, Lord Horder (1871–1955) argued that, "the stress of modern life" was a product of the "monotony and drabness" of work, a lack of exercise and sleep, an "increasing sense of international insecurity", and the "anxiety connected with the competition of living". Originally, the word stress comes from the Latin word, 'stringere- meaning to draw tight' (Arnold et al., 2005, 2010, p. 455). However, the term 'stress' was first coined by Hans Seyle (1936, 1976, p. 74), a Hungarian Canadian endocrinologist who defined it as, "the non-specific response of the body to any demand for change". In other words, Seyle's model is a response-based model because stress is the body's reaction to any emotional, psychological or physical demand. Accordingly, when an event threatens an individual's well-being, our body reacts in three stages, namely: (1) Alarm, (2) Resistance, and (3) Exhaustion.

In Stage 1, for example, upon encountering a stressor, our body reacts with a fight-or-flight response. The sympathetic nervous system is activated and hormones such as cortisol and adrenalin are released into the bloodstream to counter the stressor. In Stage 2, the body puts up resistance and the parasympathetic nervous system normalises many of the elevated physiological functions back to normal. However, blood glucose, cortisol, and adrenalin levels continue to remain at elevated levels, but the outward appearance of the human body appears to function as per normal. The

DOI: 10.4324/9781003020554-5

body remains on red alert even whilst the body appears to be normal. If the stressor continues, the body enters Stage 3 where the organism will eventually exhaust all its resources and following that, results in becoming highly susceptible to diseases and even death. These reactions are demonstrated elegantly in Nixon's (1979) and Yerkes and Dodson (1908) stress response curve (see Figure 4.1). In this illustration, we can see that stress as a form of healthy tension can improve performance. However, when the stress level reaches "Optimal activity", fatigue sets in followed by exhaustion and ill health.

Importantly, while Seyle's model was useful, it fails to distinguish between the physiological responses that we get from a stressful event such as a divorce versus a pleasant event such as receiving a promotion. Therefore, another way to look at stress is to conceptualise stress as a process whereby an individual perceives and responds to events that he or she appraises as overwhelming or threatening to his/her well-being (Lazarus & Folkman, 1984). A crucial element here is how an individual appraises a stressor to determine how he or she can respond/cope to the stressor. In other words, whether or not a stressor is experienced as stressful depends on how the individual appraises or perceives it. According to Mechanic (1978), this depends on several personal and contextual factors such as capacities, skills and abilities, constraints, resources, and norms (Mechanic, 1978).

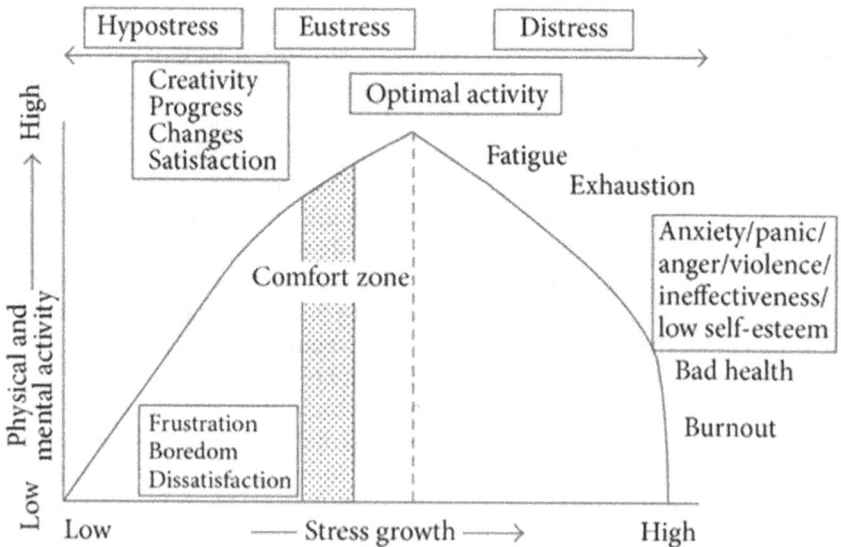

*Figure 4.1* Human response to stress curve.
Source: According to P. Nixon: Practitioner 1979, Yerkes RM, Dodson JD.

From a process perspective, stress involves two appraisal procedures (Lazarus & Folkman, 1984). The primary appraisal first determines whether the stressor poses a threat. The secondary appraisal determines if we have available resources to combat the stressor. Lazarus and Folkman (1984) discussed several possible coping mechanisms including problem-focused coping (a.k.a. active coping style) or emotion-focused coping (passive coping style; Folkman & Lazarus, 1980; Lazarus & Folkman, 1984). In addition to this, strategies for approach and avoidance-style measures of coping exist which involve assertiveness or withdrawal (Anshel, 1996; Anshel & Weinberg, 1999; Roth & Cohen, 1986). In other words, Lazarus and Folkman (1984) proposed a cognitive approach to how we evaluate stress – the idea that depending on our perceptions – a situation or event may be perceived to be threatening or not and elicit negative, positive or no stress outcomes.

**Stress as defined a Chinese context**

We would like to share an interesting fact with you regarding the meaning of stress in the Chinese language. In fact, there is no single word which can mean "stress/stressed/stressful" for all cases in the Chinese language. In the following vignette, we gave some examples of the different translations of stress within the Chinese languages. See Box 4.1 below.

---

**BOX 4.1 DIFFERENT MEANING OF STRESS WITHIN THE CHINESE LANGUAGES**

There are multiple subtle differences in how stress is represented in the Chinese language. We have provided some examples below to illustrate this.

For example, while the word 'stressful' is used in both Examples 1 and 2 below, the Chinese wording for stressful can be interpreted as 焦虑 (similar to anxious) and 紧张 (similar to excited). In contrast, in Example 3, the interpretation of "I am very stressed" translates to mean "I have a heavy burden" in the Chinese language.

What this suggests is that we should not understand stress as a one-dimensional thing. Instead, stress is a combination of cultural, social, environmental, and physical circumstances that are relevant to the individual, culture, or society. In other words, the perception and experience of stress can be subjective depending on contexts and individuals:

1  Divorce is a very stressful experience 离婚是一件很焦虑的事。
2  Teaching can be a very stressful job. 教学是一件非常紧张的工作。
3  I am very stressed. 我的压力很大。

---

**Rising stress level**

Stress levels in the workplace are rising with 6 in 10 workers in major global economies experiencing increased workplace stress. For example, in America, nearly a decade ago, 75% of adults reported experiencing moderate to high levels of stress in the past month and nearly half reported that their stress has increased in the past year (American Psychological Association, 2012).

Business consultancy, Regus (2012) surveyed 16,000 workers around the globe and found that 6 in 10 workers in significant global economies experienced increased workplace stress. The Regus survey also found that China was the most stressed country globally, with 86% of Chinese business individuals reporting a rise in stress (Regus, 2012). According to this survey, the causes of stress levels can be attributable to increased focus on the need to make money or profits, pressure from customers for better service, the demand for quarterly sales and revenues, aggressive competition from colleagues, insufficient administrative support, risk of unemployment/business failure, and loss of good staff.

A survey from Ferry (2019) also found that the overall employee stress levels have risen nearly 20% in three decades. More recently, the Australian Institute of Health and Welfare noted that the Australian Bureau of Statistics (2017–2018) reported an estimated 2.4 million Australians aged 18 and over reported high or very high levels of psychological distress (AIHW, 2020). Finally, there is also evidence that shows many employees do not take or use their annual leave. Data from Travelatte shows countries with the number of unused annual leave days from employees around the globe. While countries such as Austria, Brazil, Canada, Finland, France, Germany, Hong Kong, Norway, Spain, Thailand UAE, and UK have the highest number of leave days taken, South Koran and Japan, in terms of percentages, have among the lowest holiday leave taken. Therefore, there are great difference among different countries when it comes to holiday leaves.

**Women and stress**

Both men and women experience stress. However, there is continual debates on whether men encounter more stressors than women. What is clear is that women tend to report being more stressed out (American Psychological Association, 2012). For example, 28% of women compared to 20% men reported having a great deal of stress (8, 9, or 10 on a 10-point scale). Figures found that compared to single women (22%), married women (33%) reported experiencing a great deal of stress in the past month. Only 41% of single women compared to 56% of married women reported that their stress has increased over the past five years. Single women (63%) also reported that they feel they were able to manage their stress compared to 51% of married women.

Stress is a reaction to a change or a challenge. In the short-term, stress can be helpful in that it makes you more alert and gives you energy to get things done. However, long-term stress or chronic stress can lead to serious health problems including muscular, respiratory, cardiovascular, endocrine, gastrointestinal, nervous, and reproductive systems problems (American Psychological Association, 2018). Women are more likely than men to report stress symptoms such as tummy upset and headaches or have exacerbated conditions made worse by stress such as depression or anxiety. As far back as 2001, the National Institute of Mental Health (NIMH, 2001) in its report found that women suffered more stress than men because women have multiple roles in the home and at work. Women tend to be poor, at risk for violence and to raise their children alone; all these factors put women at more risk to be stressed out. Many more women (24%) also identified children as "a much more significant source of stress" than male respondents do (15%, APA, 2010). Things have not really changed in the department of stress and we continue to see women, especially working women working a full day of work followed by a full night of childcare and family responsibilities (Germano, 2019). That's not to say that men do not have childcare and family responsibilities, and many men are more likely to support children overnight, compared with women, but from our research, and the data that we've shared in this book, this is less common than women doing the bulk of the load in terms of managing the household and looking after children.

Recently, we conducted interviews with women about their multiple roles and how they feel about the pressures in their lives. Our study found that while times may have change, societal norms and expectation about what an ideal woman should be like in private, and in public, have remained stubbornly inflexible. For instance, many interviewed women reported that they do the lion's share of the housework despite working full-time. These norms continue to exert great influence over women's multiple roles and the pressures women experienced. Consequently, many women continue to try to do it and to have it all. The following excerpts demonstrate some of the pressure women experienced.

> A lot of pressure to perform and not be seen as doing 'less than' childless colleagues.
>
> I try very hard not to put pressure on myself, but at times I do feel I am spinning a lot of plates and doing a lot of things. This makes me feel spread too thin and quality at times for what I am not giving my kids or my work, etc.
>
> A fair amount of pressure to keep on top of tasks. I know I have done a good job if everything gets attended to and everyone has their needs met.

## Stress triggers

It is important to note that stress is a normal response to physical, mental or emotional changes and not something in our head. If stress or chronic stress is not managed appropriately, it can cause high blood pressure, headaches, insomnia, difficulty concentrating, muscular pain, and exacerbate anxiety and/or depression. Consequently, it is important for us to identify triggers of stress.

In the first instance, it is important to distinguish between acute stress responses and chronic stress responses. Acute stress responses occur when out heart beats faster and our breathing becomes rapid as our body pumps adrenaline. Chronic stress occurs when we are under constant stress and our body exhausts all its resources. At this stage, we become highly susceptible to diseases or becoming ill. Furthermore, we may feel stressed in response to some external or internal triggers including some of the following stressors: personal or family crisis, small daily hassles (e.g., traffic jams), loud noise(s), loneliness, loss of control, natural disaster (e.g., flood), divorce/separation, death in the family, mortgage stress, etc. Stress in many ways is an individualised experience. What may be stressful to one person may not be stressful to another person. Individuals' past experiences, other stressors in our life and even genetics can affect what and how we experience potential stressors. Therefore, it is important that we in our busy life try to slow down and identify what could be the trigger for our stress.

## How men and women cope with stress

Stress is an inevitable consequence of living in our modern world. Regardless of what triggers the emotional or physical responses to stressors, men and women report different ways of managing stress (APA, 2010). According to a study conducted by the APA (2010), both men and women cope with stress through sedentary activities such as reading, listening to music, and watching television to manage their stress rather than undertaking more healthier behaviours like seeing a mental health professional and/or exercising.

However, 16% of the male participants were more likely than female participants (4%) to play sports to relieve their stress (APA, 2010). Approximately 52% of male participants stated they would listen to music compared to 47% of female participants (APA, 2010). Moreover, approximately 9% of men were also more likely than women (4%) to report that they will do nothing to manage their stress. Significantly more women (35%) than men (24%) reported that they exercised only once a week or less. The reasons women gave for not exercising more often than men were that they were just too tired (39% vs. 26%). This is not surprising when you considered that many women not only work but also have the lion's share of housework responsibilities. In contrast, men were more likely than women to state that they exercise because it provided them with something to do (34% vs. 23%), keeps them from becoming unwell or sick (29% vs. 18%), and sport is something they are good at (19% vs. 11%, APA, 2010).

We found in our interviews insights as to why women did not exercise more regularly. For example:

> I maintain a fortnightly personal training session and try to do other at home sessions between but often fail due to [shift work].

I used to, but pregnancy has done a number on my ability to exercise. Less so currently as I'm heavily pregnant, but when I'm not pregnant, I make a real effort to exercise.

The APA study also reported that women (31%) are more likely than men (21%) to use eating as a way of managing their stress. As a result, many women reported that they have engaged in unhealthy eating in the past month far more often than men (49% of women vs. 30% of men). Women were far more likely than men to say they read to manage stress (57% vs. 34%) and overall, tend to report more stress management activities that connect them with other people, like spending time with friends or family (54% vs. 39%) and going to church or religious services (27% vs. 18%).

Finally, both male and female participants admitted that the lack of willpower acts as a barrier against them making the lifestyle and behaviour changes recommended by a healthcare provider (34% vs. 24%). When asked what they need to change their willpower, women were more likely than men to say they needed more energy/to be less fatigued (56% vs. 44%) and needed greater confidence in their ability to improve their willpower (60% vs. 38%). Finally, the report found that six times as many women as men say that having more help with household chores would allow them to improve their willpower (23% vs. 4%).

## How can women better manage stress?

There are several things women can do to manage stress. First and foremost, we must acknowledge that our needs should be a part of how we care for ourselves and that we should not feel guilty about practising healthy self-care strategies nor should we feel guilty about taking time out to engage with these strategies. It does appear to be crazy that when we are surrounded by modern appliances that can wash and dry our clothes, vacuum our floors, and heat up pre-packaged meals, we crave personal time more than ever. Modern living has its own drawbacks with time-consuming and sometimes pointless activities such as engaging with Email, Twitter, and Facebook. These can steal from us more time than is necessary in every living day. We hope the strategies suggested below can provide you with some ideas on your needs and areas in your life that you might want to improve. We would like to emphasise that these are merely our suggestions for some 'me-time' rather than a list of 'must do' things.

## Take time out to reflect

How do you feel physically, emotionally, and mentally? How do you feel about your occupational, social, and spiritual life? Is there anything you would do differently in the following 6 areas – paying special attention to what you would do to achieve balance in those areas.

### Physical state

Regular exercise is vital. Try to find at least half an hour each day to do some jogging, running, or walking. If walking or jogging is not your cup of tea, then try some relaxation techniques such as yoga, meditation, or listen to relaxing music. Part of being physically healthy is to eat healthy (for example, following the Mediterranean diet). Try not to binge eat. Rather, organise and pack snacks in small quantities that you can graze on throughout the day. Schedule leisure time (and switch off that mobile phone) and try to get about 7 to 9 hours of sleep per night.

### Emotional and mental state

As humans, we do feel sad at times. There is nothing wrong if you want to have a cry because something negative has happened at work or home or just in our day-to-day life. It is healthy to express your emotions. However, it is important not to dwell too long in this negative state. Rather, engage in positive emotion and repeat these positive emotions to ensure a healthy self-esteem. Mindfulness is one such technique. Mindfulness refers to a psychological state of awareness that arises through paying attention, on purpose, in the present moment and being non-judgemental (Kabat-Zinn, 2017). In other words, mindfulness practices help us to focus our attention, thoughts and feelings without judgement. In doing so, we are better able to regulate our negative emotions, decrease our stress, anxiety, and depression.

Research over the past decade has consistently demonstrated that mindfulness is connected to much improved metacognitive awareness, reduced rumination, less emotional reactivity, diminished stress, enhanced attentional capacities, and improved working memory (Farb et al., 2010; Jha et al., 2010; Moore & Malinowski, 2009). All these cognitive gains contribute to effective emotion-regulation strategies. Being mindful also allows us to focus on gratitude and to stay in the present moment. This will guide against negativity which can lead to stress and more anxiety.

### Occupational state

In your job, establish achievable goals and set time limits for each task. It is important to clarify the boundaries between work and home so that proper boundaries can be set up. This can be really difficult when one works from home especially during the COVID-19 pandemic where the days seem to simply blend into each other. Our suggestion is to set a time period and stop when it is time to stop. A reward such as a piece of chocolate or a glass of wine makes this process easier. However, a note of caution in moderation (e.g., wine and chocolate) is called for here.

## Social state

We are social beings. Quoting Aristotle, the legendary ancient Greek philosopher, "Man is by nature a social animal; an individual who is unsocial naturally and not accidentally is either beneath our notice or more than human. Society is something that precedes the individual". Therefore, it is important for us to maintain loving relationships, remain connected with our friends and establish healthy boundaries with others.

### *Spirituality state*

Spirituality is not just about an individual's religious practice or creed. It has more to do with one's sense of peace and purpose. It can be about the process of developing beliefs about the meaning of life and our connections with others, without any set of religious values. Meaning is important because it provides a purpose for our lives (Frankl, 1978). Meaning provides values and standards we can use to judge our actions. Meaning also gives us control over the events in our lives and finally, meaning equips us with self-worth. When people are unable to find meaning in their lives, they become easily distressed (Frankl, 1978).

In his book, Man's search for meaning, Viktor Frankl, the great psychiatrist and an Auschwitz death camp survivor, described his life in Nazi death camps, and the stories from his patients to argue that while we cannot avoid suffering, we can choose how to cope with it, find meaning in it, and move forward with renewed purpose. For Frankl, meaning for him personally is about acting as a psychiatrist and physician to his fellow prisoners, as well as reflecting on the love he had for his wife, Tilly. The following passage from his book illustrates this sense of meaningfulness eloquently:

> We stumbled on in the darkness.... The accompanying guards kept shouting at us and driving us with the butts of their rifles.... Hiding his mouth behind his upturned collar, the man marching next to me whispered suddenly: "If our wives could see us now! I do hope they are better off in their camps and don't know what is happening to us." That brought thoughts of my own wife to mind.... my mind clung to my wife's image, imagining it with an uncanny acuteness. I heard her answering me, saw her smile, her frank and encouraging look.... I understood how a man who has nothing left in this world still may know bliss, be it only for a brief moment, in the contemplation of his beloved.

The approaches above have important benefits for one's physical and mental health. They should be considered foundational building blocks for a healthy lifestyle. Finally, consider using a personal wellness plan because it can be tailored specifically to your needs. These are just a few practical steps you can take to start your personalised wellness plan. Being able to have a wellness plan tailored to your specific needs is important because we know we will continue to experience stress in different phases of our lives. Developing a personal wellness plan with built-in recovery phase and self-care along different phases may help us handle stress in a manageable way. The success we build along the way means that we can empower ourselves to make the necessary adjustments so that we can build up a healthy lifestyle.

## Reference list

American Psychological Association (2018). Stress effects on the body. Retrieved from https://www.apa.org/topics/stress-body.

American Psychological Association (2010). Gender and stress. Retrieved from https://www.apa.org/news/press/releases/stress/2010/gender-stress.

Anshel, M. H. (1996). Coping styles among adolescent competitive athletes. *The Journal of Social Psychology, 136*(3), 311–323. doi:10.1080/00224545.1996.9714010.

Anshel, M. H., & Weinberg, R. T. (1999). Re-examining coping among basketball referees following stressful events: Implications for coping interventions. *Journal of Sport Behavior, 22*(2), 144–161.

Arnold, J., Silvester, J., Patterson, F., Robertson, I., Cooper, C., & Burnes, B. (2005). *Work psychology: Understanding human behaviour in workplace.* Essex: Prentice Hall.

Arnold, J., Randall, R., Patterson, F., Sylvester, J., Robertson, I., Cooper, C., Burnes, B., Swailes, S., Harris, D., Axxtell, C., & Den Hartog, D. (2010). *Work physiology: Understanding human behaviour in the workplace*, 5th ed. Harlow: Pearson Education.

Australian Institute of Health and Welfare (2020). Stress and trauma. Retrieved from https://www.aihw.gov.au/reports/australias-health/stress-and-trauma. Farb, N. A. S., Anderson, A. K., Mayberg, H., Bean, J., McKeon, D., & Segal, Z. V. (2010). Minding one's emotions: Mindfulness training alters the neural expression of sadness. *Emotion, 10*, 25–33. doi:10.1037/a0017151.supp. Ferry, K. (2019). Workplace stress continues to mount. Retrieved from https://www.kornferry.com/insights/articles/workplace-stress-motivation.

Folkman, S., & Lazarus, R.S. (1980). An analysis of coping in a middle-aged community sample. *Journal of Health & Social Behavior, 21*(3), 219–239.

Frankl, V. (1978). *The unheard cry for meaning.* New York: Simon & Schuster.

Germano, M. (2019). Women are working more than ever, but they still take on most household responsibilities. Retrieved from https://www.forbes.com/sites/maggiegermano/2019/03/27/women-are-working-more-than-ever-but-they-still-take-on-most-household-responsibilities/?sh=e107f1352e9e

Jha, A. P., Stanley, E. A., Kiyonaga, A., Wong, L., & Gelfand, L. (2010). Examining the protective effects of mindfulness training on working memory capacity and affective experience. *Emotion, 10*, 54–64. doi:10.1037/a0018438.

Kabat-Zinn, J. (2017). Too early to tell: The potential impact and challenges—Ethical and otherwise—Inherent in the mainstreaming of Dharma in an increasingly dystopian world. *Mindfulness, 8*, 1125–1135. doi:10.1007/s12671-017-0758-2.

Lazarus, R. S., & Folkman, S. (1984). *Stress, appraisal and coping.* New York: Springer.

Mechanic, D. (1978). *Students under stress: A study in the social psychology of adaptation*. Madison: University of Wisconsin Press.

Moore, A., & Malinowski, P. (2009). Meditation, mindfulness and cognitive flexibility. *Consciousness and Cognition, 18*, 176–186. doi:10.1016/j.concog.2008.12.008.

Nixon, P. (1979). The performance level: Arousal stress. Adapted from P. Nixon, Practitioner, 1979. *World Applied Science Journal, 19*, 1381–1387.

National Institute of Mental Health (2001). Women hold up half the sky: Women and mental health research. NIH Publication No. 01-4607.

Regus (2012). Regus work life-balance index. Retrieved from https://www.slideshare.net/REGUSmedia/regus-worklife-balance-white-paper.

Roth, S., & Cohen, L. J. (1986). Approach, avoidance, and coping with stress. *American Psychologist, 41*(7), 813–819. doi:10.1037/0003-066X.41.7.813

Selye, H. (1936). A syndrome produced by diverse nocuous agents. *Nature, 138*, 32. doi:10.1038/138032a0.

Selye, H. (1976) *Stress in health and disease*. Boston, MA: Butterworths.

Yerkes, R. M., & Dodson, J. D. (1908). The relation of strength of stimulus to rapidity of habit-formation. *Journal of Comparative Neurology and Psychology, 18*, 459–482.

# 5 Rushing and reaching breaking point

Nature does not hurry, yet everything is accomplished.

—Lao Tzu

In one of the largest surveys of its kind, the UK Household Longitudinal Survey which examined 6,025 participants reported what most working mothers already know, that working mothers are 18% more stressed than other people and this percentage rises to 40% for working mothers with two children (Ramaswamy, 2019). Although we do have official statistics, we suspect that this percentage is even higher for single mothers. According to the Household, Income and Labour Dynamics (HILDA) survey in Australia, working mothers in full-time jobs have the highest 'work-family conflict' levels. While most women report rushing, given these statistics, this chapter focuses specifically on modern working women (Gartry & Lloyd, 2019) and how they 'rush' about in their daily lives to get things done.

As modern working mothers with children, we always seem to be rushing around doing one thing to the next with a never-ending to-do list that keeps us from catching our breath. We cannot remember the last time we watched the sunset with our spouses or partners. There are times when we think we should really slow down and take a break, but this becomes a struggle as well. Many women who share these experiences understand: the constant struggle to meet work deadlines, financial responsibilities, household duties, caretaker obligations, and demands of intimate relationships. At the end of the day, all these responsibilities and duties weigh heavily on working mothers who often find themselves out of breath.

In her book, "Rushing woman's syndrome: The impact of a never-ending to-do list and how to stay healthy in today's busy world", Dr Libby Weaver describes the term, 'Rushing Woman's Syndrome (RWS)' as a modern condition of always being 'busy, busy, busy'. According to Weaver (2017), the impact of a constant state of rushing can adversely affect women's health and create havoc with their hormones. You know you have RWS when someone asks you how you are and you instinctively respond with, "I am

DOI: 10.4324/9781003020554-6

busy", or "I am stressed". Women experiencing RWS have described the need to be on top of things, to squeeze as many things as one can into a day and to not let anyone down even if it means staying up after midnight to answer emails. This state of rushing has become the norm for many modern working women who are juggling career/work, families, and social responsibilities. In other words, modern working women rush to cope with what they need to do on a daily basis. However, this permanent state of stress can create hormone imbalances which can contribute to adverse menopausal issues later in life.

In an article in *Today*, Coffey and Abrahamson (2020) reported on how the coronavirus crisis took a greater toll on women, especially on mothers, than on fathers. Many women who worked from home also had the added pressure of homeschooling their children. This dual role means women carry heavy "mental loads" – the emotional and psychological burden of making sure they have academic work ready for their children to work on, remembering to pick up milk from the grocery store, checking that the second load of washing goes into the dryer, making sure they have booked in to see the doctor and other various little 'details and things' they have to do around and outside the house. For mothers who are now working from home, this stress is compounded by having to attend to Zoom meetings, discussing project details with their clients and completing tasks their supervisors have assigned them from their home laptop. For some men, they oversaw this, too, but the women we spoke to indicated that their male partners seemed better at closing the door and not getting interrupted during their Zoom meetings. Men also seem to carry much less of the burden at home, so it is no wonder that countless "things they have to do" keep women up at night. This is also true for women without children. In our interviews, women without children reported that they experienced a heavier 'mental load' burden compared to their husbands or partners.

In Australia, men are doing an extra hour of housework per week compared to what they did 14 years ago (Wilkins & Lass, 2018). This is good news, but married women with children still undertake approximately 60% more of the housework and caring for dependants (Wilkins & Lass, 2018). Similarly, researchers in England surveyed 3,591 two-parent opposite sex families and found that mothers took on more childcare and housework responsibilities than fathers who had the same work arrangements during the COVID-19 lockdown (Andrew et al., 2020; ITV news, 2020). Statistics from the Organisation for Economic Co-operation and Development (OECD, 2021) confirm that women spend more time in unpaid work such as housework and childcare. The table below summarises the time men and women spend in unpaid work in different OECD and non-OECD countries. What the table reveals is that in both OECD and non-OECD countries, women spend more time in unpaid work compared to men. This difference

*Table 5.1* Time spent in unpaid work by gender in age group (15–64) in 2020

| Country | | Men (minutes/day) | Women (minutes/day) |
|---|---|---|---|
| Australia | | 171.6 | 311.0 |
| Austria | | 135.3 | 269.2 |
| Belgium | | 144.2 | 237.3 |
| Canada | | 148.1 | 223.7 |
| Denmark | | 186.1 | 242.8 |
| Estonia | | 160.2 | 249.2 |
| Finland | | 157.5 | 235.8 |
| France | | 134.9 | 224.0 |
| Germany | | 150.4 | 242.3 |
| Greece | | 95.1 | 259.5 |
| Hungary | | 162.3 | 293.8 |
| Ireland | | 127.0 | 292.5 |
| Italy | | 130.7 | 306.3 |
| Japan | | 40.8 | 224.3 |
| South Korea | | 49.0 | 215.0 |
| Latvia | | 129.7 | 253.3 |
| Lithuania | | 151.6 | 292.0 |
| Luxembourg | | 121.1 | 239.6 |
| Mexico | | 131.4 | 331.3 |
| Netherlands | | 145.4 | 224.9 |
| New Zealand | | 141.0 | 264.0 |
| Norway | | 168.5 | 227.4 |
| Poland | | 158.8 | 295.0 |
| Portugal | | 96.3 | 328.2 |
| Slovenia | | 166.5 | 286.2 |
| Spain | | 145.9 | 289.1 |
| Sweden | | 171.0 | 220.2 |
| Turkey | | 67.6 | 305.0 |
| United Kingdom | | 140.1 | 248.6 |
| United States | | 145.0 | 241.0 |
| OECD – average | | 135.8 | 262.4 |
| Non-OECD economies | China (People's Republic of) | 91.0 | 234.0 |
| | India | 51.8 | 351.9 |
| | South Africa | 102.9 | 249.6 |

Source: Organisation for Economic Cooperation and Development (OECD, 2021). Stat https://stats.oecd.org/index.aspx?queryid=54757.

is particularly striking between men and women in Japan, South Korea, and India suggesting the lack of appropriately balanced economic conditions for these women. Refer to this in Table 5.1.

In the next section of this chapter, we would like to share with you the lives of two busy women. The first is that of Sharon and her morning routine (See Box 5.1). The second is that of Samara, a migrant woman and her experiences back in her hometown of Pakistan (See Box 5.2).

## BOX 5.1 SHARON'S BUSY MORNING ROUTINE

Sharon is a 35-year-old woman living with her husband and two children in Singapore. Her husband is an accountant with a global financial agency and Sharon is a teacher at her local government primary school. Her two children, Jane (8) and Jack (7) also attend the local government primary school. We asked Sharon to share her morning routine with us.

Sharon reported that,

> I usually start my "morning routine" the night before because I have to work in the morning. This has become a habit and it is easy for me to coordinate my work outfit the night before. I also pack my workbag (phone, makeup kit, water and snacks) so I can grab it on the way out. I lay out my son's and daughter's clothes, socks, and school bags the night before in their room. However, I have been getting them to this themselves because I want them to take some responsibilities.

The following is a schedule of Sharon's morning routine.

Wake up at 6:00am

6:00–6:10 Go straight to the bathroom and start brushing my teeth, wash face, moisturise and get dressed.

6:10–6:25 Quickly put on make-up. If there is no time for make-up at home, I sometimes put my makeup on the ride to work.

6:30 Go into kitchen and start making breakfast for my husband and children. I like to cook a warm nutritious breakfast for them in the morning. I also start making the kids' lunch boxes and water bottles.

7:00 Wake the kids up. This can take some time and effort because my children are not morning "little people". In between waking them and making breakfast, I sometimes lose my temper and I will shout at my husband to get the kids out of bed.

7:15–7:30 Breakfast time for all

7:30–7:40 I clean up breakfast table. Husband is off to work by now.

7:50 Check children and get them ready for school.

7:55–8:00 Grab my bag and rush out the door with the kids!

"As you can see, we are on a pretty tight schedule. Unlike my husband who wakes up leisurely with his cup of tea, I am the one who has to cook breakfast and get the kids ready. I also have to pack the kids' lunch boxes! I have given up asking my husband to help in the morning because things will NOT get done on time and we will be late. I do not want my children or myself to be late in the morning".

**BOX 5.2 SAMARA AND HER STRUGGLE WITH CAREER AMBITION AS WELL AS HOUSEHOLD RESPONSIBILITIES**

Samara is a 40-year-old woman with three children. She and her husband migrated to Australia six years ago. Her husband has a part-time job and Samara works on a sessional basis. Samara is also currently undertaking additional training to become a counsellor. Samara's daily life revolves around her family, work, and training.

We asked Samara if she is happy to share her life experiences back in her hometown with us and she gladly said yes. Samara talked about her ambition in wanting to become an academic because she had a marvellous mentor when she was in university. This is the story of Samara.

"I have often wondered how things would have been different if I was a less ambitious individual. I am in my forties and I started my career as an academic 22 years ago. I did not have any distractions at that time and all I had to do was to focus on my career and manage the home.

"However, I reached breaking point in attempting to manage it all. In my culture, the most important thing for a woman is being a mother, a daughter and a good wife. But I wanted to work outside. While I appreciate my home-maker role, work is intellectually satisfying for me and this gives me an important sense of purpose in my life.

"It was a hard choice but looking back now, I realised it has been very stressful. I live in a society that had demanding and set expectations of women. Therefore, I grew up believing I have to be a perfect mother, daughter, wife, and daughter-in-law. I soon realised that I was unable to cope with all the expectations my family, employers, and society expects of me.

"As a consequence, I often feel overwhelmed with what I had to do on a daily basis. I had health issues as a result and even though I have now managed to cope with this issue, my health problems persisted. I wish I had known earlier about the importance of looking after myself and my health. The physical impact of spreading myself too thin took a toll on my psychological and physical health. My emotional well-being was also affected and I felt fragile all the time.

"My feelings of despair were further compounded by my sense of self-doubt and guilt as a woman. These feelings stayed with me for a long time and I questioned my ability to work both as an employee and as a mother. The most important lesson I learned through my life experience was not to take life as a linear equation without rest. I should have learned not to rush about so much."

We believe Sharon's morning routine may be shared by many other working mothers. However, we suspect that Asian working mothers may be slightly worst off. A study conducted by the Ministry of Gender Equality and Family along with Statistics Korea found that South Korean working mothers spent nearly two hours more on housework and childcare than their spouses compared to the 31 minutes/day Korean men spend on housework. In contrast, Australian, Canadian, and New Zealand women did about three hours of housework, but their partners supported them by taking care of the home for one hour and 50 minutes. This approximates to four times more than South Korean men.

Samara's life experiences reflect the continued challenges among many Asian women faced in their juggle between work and household responsibilities. In many Asian countries, there are strict norms, rules, and regulations about how women should think, feel, and behave at home and in the workplace (i.e., for those who are allowed to work outside).

## Gender roles and stereotypes

We live in societies that have a set of ideas about how men and women should think, behave, dress, and present ourselves. Gender roles relate to expectations around how men and women should behave, dress, talk, and conduct themselves according to their assigned sex. For example, girls and women are generally expected to dress in feminine ways and to be courteous, nurturing, and accommodating. In contrast, men are expected to act strong and be assertive or aggressive (Hodges & Budig, 2010). While expectations around gender roles are shifting, particularly in Western cultures, there are still underpinning stereotypes and beliefs residing in one's subconscious.

All cultures and societies have gender role expectations about how men and women should think and behave. While these expectations can vary between groups and may change over time, there is an expectation that members in that culture know what is expected of them. The following provides some examples of these gender stereotypes:

- Gender stereotypes based on personality traits. For instance, women should be nurturing and sensitive in their dealings with others. In contrast, men are usually self-confident and bold in how they interact with others. This results in stereotypes in parenting or other carer responsibilities which results in assumptions in the workplace. For example, when a strong woman makes an unpopular decision, workplace gossip may call her a bitch, while a man may be deemed to "have it all under control" when he makes an unpopular decision.
- Domestic responsibilities – Women are expected to take care of both household chores and children, while men are expected to be the breadwinner of the household. These attitudes are shifting in Western

culture, with increasing numbers of females becoming the main or sole breadwinner.

- Jobs – Some people have the stereotype that teachers and nurses are women while pilots and engineers are men. This can influence imagery used in magazine articles, news stories, etc., as well as influence career advice given to girls and boys. Harvard University's Implicit Bias test around gender is enlightening, and a good way to understand where your gender-based biases may lie.
- Physical appearance – women are expected to be slender and graceful, while men are expected to be tall and muscular. Men should wear pants while women are expected to dress in a feminine way. Women are also more likely to be judged for their clothing choices compared to men.

Some of these extreme gender stereotypes can harm us because they do not allow us to be ourselves. For this reason, it is important for us to break down these stereotypes so that we can be ourselves.

## Unequal household responsibilities

According to the Australian Bureau of Statistics, the typical Australian woman spends between five and 14 hours a week doing unpaid domestic housework. In contrast, the typical Australian man reportedly spends under 5 hours a week doing housework, suggesting that women are doing the lion's share of housework and childcare responsibilities. This is an issue plaguing many women around the globe. For instance, according to the International Labour Organisation (ILO, 2016), women continue to disproportionately bear the burden of unpaid work across the world. In fact, unpaid care and domestic work is valued to be between 10% and 39% of the Gross Domestic Product around the globe.

## Women and their expectations

We grew up in societies that have certain expectations of us. For example, single women are expected to marry and have children. But this expectation is slowly changing and according to Graham, Hill, Shelly, and Takat (2013), there are several reasons why many Australian women may decide not to have children such as never really wanting to have children, not being in the 'right' relationship and being in a relationship where their partner did not want to have any children. There is also an expectation that women can (and should expect to) have it all – maintain a career, study, raise children, and manage the household. However, the ideal of a perfect woman and a perfect mother is very difficult to achieve. Indeed, Meeussen and Van Laar (2018) found that the pressure to be a perfect mother was positively related to parental burnout. Meeussen and Van Laar (2018) also found that mothers who felt that they have to be perfect in both family and work responsibilities experienced poorer work-family balance which affected their personal lives as well as career ambitions.

Modern women not only have high expectations of themselves, but they also struggle to achieve those expectations. We are expected to be able to do our jobs with the same amount of time and energy irrespective of whether we have childcare responsibilities. We are expected to have our house always be clean and tidy; that our children are socially, emotionally, physically, and behaviourally perfect and that we continued to maintain a level of physical attractiveness that society deems acceptable even when we have a cold. It is no wonder that many women ended up feeling rushed and stressed.

## The way forward

There is a great saying, "hurry spoil curry" – if we rush around, we can easily make a mistake along the way. This happened to Sharon, whose example was shared earlier in the chapter. Sharon was rushing to get her children up, to cook a hot breakfast, to pack her children's lunches but ended up snapping at her husband. It might have been better for everyone if Sharon's children get their own bowl of cereal or eat a couple of pieces of toast. But this may not suit Sharon because she grew up with expectations that a good mother is one who cooks a hot breakfast for her family. While we cannot advise what Sharon should or should not do for breakfast, we can offer some coping techniques that might help busy working mothers. Again, these are suggestions rather than a must do list.

Some suggested coping techniques for busy women:

1   Change your perceptions and modify your expectations.

It is important that we pay attention to both our mental and physical health. We need to be mindful about how we are feeling. For example, do you feel anxious, impatient, or tense all the time? If you do, then consider taking time out to calm your mind or go for a walk to release some of that tension.

2   Prioritise and delegate.

We should accept that we are not indispensable and that we all need help sometimes. There is no harm in asking for help. Learning to delegate family responsibilities to other members in the family is an important skill to have. Similarly, learning to delegate work responsibilities to other staff members at work is also important because it builds trust and cooperation.

If the work task cannot be delegated, then make a list and prioritise what needs to be done first. It is ok to say no to something that is not 100% urgent. Then hand off what you can to qualified people you trust. This will save you time and allow you to focus on real priorities and your expertise.

3    Identify challenges, benefits, and consider the big picture.

Identify what is at risk and what you have to gain, and if the work task is indeed important, then approach the task with diligence. Reframing the job in terms of how it gets you closer to your goals; that is, connecting with the "why" can help you see the job for its real value and enjoy the process, as well.

This principle applies to household responsibilities too. For example, what is the risk of not making up the bed every morning? The risk may be that if your mother-in-law drops by, she may be upset to see an unmade bed. Next, identify how much of an impact this risk is for you? If this risk is very impactful, then consider what strategies or who you can delegate this task to? For instance, this may be a good opportunity to teach your children, husband, or other family members the importance of sharing the housework. Now to share a little secret with you all, one of the authors of this book reports that she never spends time making the beds. Why you may ask, well according to this author, this is because her mother-in-law lives in a different country, far far away.

4    Compartmentalise the task into timed segments.

A useful way to handle tasks is to break them into manageable segments. For example, break the job up into smaller parts and focus on each task for a specific amount of time. Reward yourself after completing a set of tasks or take a break. By doing this, you can look forward to the easier part of the task.

5    Limit distractions.

Many of us become easily distracted in our work and at home. Therefore, you may wish to limit these distractions. For example, you may set a time to check all morning emails at 11am and then a final email check at 4:30pm. This way, you will not be distracted into other tasks that are not prioritised. Another idea is to close the door to your office or set up a working space where the kids are not allowed to go in when you are there. If the kids are at home with you, make sure they are assigned some tasks to do, such as completing some mathematical problems on the computers or working online with their teacher. These strategies should buy you some time to attend to a Zoom meeting. Then, there is always the strategy of turning off the camera in your virtual Zoom or Team meeting. This is useful especially if you need to drag one of your kids out of your office or sign for a parcel delivery.

## Reference list

Andrew, A., Cattan, S., Costa Dias, M., Farquharson, C., Kraftman, L., Krutikova, S., Phimister, A., & Sevilla, A. (27 May 2020). How are mothers and fathers balancing work and family under lockdown? Retrieved from https://www.ifs.org.uk/publications/14860.

Coffey, L. T., & Abrahamson, R. P. (2020). Why mothers are bearing such a huge mental load during coronavirus pandemic. Retrieved from https://www.today.com/parents/mental-load-coronavirus-pandemic-means-moms-take-more-t179021.

Gartry, L., & Lloyd, M. (2019). Working mothers more stressed than fathers as cost of childcare skyrockets, HILDA survey shows. *ABC News*. Retrieved from https://www.abc.net.au/news/2019-07-30/working-mothers-more-stressed-than-fathers-report-finds/11365632.

Graham, M., Hill, E., Shelly, J., & Taket, A. (2013). Why are childless women childless? Findings from an exploratory study in Victoria, Australia. *Journal of Social Inclusion, 4*(1), 70–89.

Hodges, J. M., & Budig, J. M. (2010). Who gets the daddy bonus? Organizational hegemonic masculinity and the impact of fatherhood on earnings. *Gender and Society, 24*(6), 717–745.

Meeussen, L., & Van Laar, C. (2018). Feeling pressure to be a perfect mother relates to parental burnout and career ambitions. *Frontiers in Psychology, 9*, 2113. doi:10.3389/fpsyg.2018.02113.

Organisation for Economic Co-operation and Development (OECD, 2021). Employment: Time spent in paid and unpaid work, by sex. Retrieved from https://stats.oecd.org/index.aspx?queryid=54757.

Ramaswamy, C. (2019). It is a scandal that working mothers are 40% more stressed than other people. *The Guardian*. Retrieved from https://www.theguardian.com/lifeandstyle/2019/jan/28/scandal-working-mothers-40-per-cent-more-stressed-other-people.

Weaver, L., Dr (2017). *Rushing woman's syndrome: The impact of a never-ending to-do list and how to stay healthy in today's busy world*. Frankfurt am Main: Hay House.

Wilkins, R., & Lass, I. (2018). The Household, Income and Labour Dynamics in Australia (HILDA) survey: Selected findings from waves 1 to 16. Retrieved from https://melbourneinstitute.unimelb.edu.au/__data/assets/pdf_file/0005/2839919/2018-HILDA-SR-for-web.pdf.

Women at Work, Trends (2016). International Labour Organization: Women's economic empowerment in the changing world of work. Report of the Secretary-General, E/CN.6/2017/3, December 2016. Retrieved from https://interactive.unwomen.org/multimedia/infographic/changingworldofwork/en/index.html.

# 6 Diversity

There is no limit to what we, as women, can accomplish.

—Michelle Obama

Women are heterogeneous. We are influenced and affected by a variety of societal and cultural factors, genetic differences, and experiences. Society is full of diverse experiences and backgrounds, from people of different sexualities and genders, through to people of different cultural backgrounds, including First Nations people. Neurodiversity, and other differences are also important to consider. This chapter could only touch on some of this – You will hear the voices of Chinese women who were forced to have their feet crushed in the name of beauty. You will also hear the cry of a Muslim migrant woman daring to have a career and a woman who identifies as having Autism Spectrum Disorder (ASD). In telling us their stories, these women are breaking the silence around some of these 'taboo' topics and through their voices, we hope they can start to heal themselves. We will begin with foot binding, a practice that was done to thousands of Chinese women many, many years ago, and all in the name of beauty. In many ways, foot binding shares many parallels with women who undergo breast augmentation surgery, both are focused on certain female body parts which are defined as sexual and their augmentation is undertaken to provide sexual pleasure for men and women. According to Dettwyler (1995), there is a correlation between foot binding and breast augmentation because both were about changing women's bodies and appearance to please others, usually men. In addition, both impacted women's abilities to experience the world, to live well and to function.

Foot binding was said to have started in China from about the tenth century. It was a Chinese custom of breaking and binding young girls' feet to modify the shape and size of their feet. Having dainty little feet was considered a status symbols for wealth and a mark of beauty. These bound feet were known as lotus feet. However, this practice of applying tight wrapping to restrict young girls' feet to alter their growth was extremely painful.

DOI: 10.4324/9781003020554-7

More horribly, this was often done on girls of about three to five years old when their feet were still soft enough to be broken, healed and rebroken. As women, it breaks our hearts to imagine how these little girls must have cried as their feet were broken by their loved ones. In traditional China, the bound feet symbolise a woman's identity, virtue, stature, and feminism. In reality, foot binding was a form of body modification, in many ways it mirrors the experience of body modification women use today (see Dettwyler, 1995). The following boxed example (Box 6.1) illustrates what goes on behind the process of foot binding.

---

### BOX 6.1 THE PRACTICE OF FOOT BINDING

A mother or grandmother would begin the foot binding process with the clipping of the toenails and the soaking of the feet either in hot water or in a concoction of ingredients including various herbs and nuts to soften the tissue of the foot in order to facilitate manipulation. The feet are also massaged and doused with alum. All the toes on the foot, except the big one, are broken and folded under the sole. The toes are then bound in place with a 10' × 12" silk or cotton bandage. Every two days, these wrappings are removed for washing and meticulous manicuring of the toenails occurs to avoid infection. The arch of the foot is also broken and the foot is pulled straight with the leg. Gradually, the sizes of the shoe are also reduced in order to accommodate the shrinking feet. To encourage the feet to achieve the desired shape, girls are made to walk long distances so that their own weight crushes their feet into shape. The flesh of the foot would also be lacerated, or sharp objects may be inserted in the bandage to encourage 'excess' flesh to rot away so that smaller feet may be achieved. In earlier years, the washing and binding is carried out by the mother. As time passes, the girls themselves tighten their bandages on their own. At the end of two years of excruciating pain, a pair of tiny folded feet is seen. To make sure that the toes stay in place, this foot binding process is carried out for an additional ten years (Mao, 2007).

One can only imagine the excruciating pain these girls must have had to endure at the tender age of between three to five years old. Accompanying the pain are physical problems. As Miltner (1937) noted, the pain was exacerbated by infections which inevitably arose, in many cases causing gangrene, and circulatory, ligament and bone damage. Foot binding was officially banned in 1912 by the new Republic of China government, but this was not actively implemented and some women continued to do it in secret (Ko, 2007).

**Theories about foot binding**

There are a number of theories about foot binding. According to historian Dorothy Ko, foot binding was seen as a necessary part of being feminine and civilised. Fred Blake, an anthropologist argued that foot binding was a type of discipline undertaken and perpetuated by women as a means of reinforcing women's status and role (Blake, 1994).

Other theorists see foot binding as an oppressive, violent and sexist practice against women because the binding restricted movement, rendering these women dependent on their families, particularly on their husband when they married (Hong, 1997;O'Toole & Schiffman, 1997; Renzetti et al., 2008; Stewart, 2014). The Chinese feminist, Qiu Jin argued that foot binding made women subservient, stuck indoors with these bound feet that affected mobility. Hong (1997) argued

*Figure 6.1* Young girls with bound feet practice the Beijing Opera at a theatre school in Beijing in 1934.
Source: Public Domain.

ending the practice of foot binding was a step towards female emancipation in China.

There are parallels with the ways women's bodies are augmented today. In her famous work on the topic, Kathy Dettwyler argued that many in the west view the practice of foot binding as barbaric and reductive, cruel and bizarre. However, as she notes, the use of breast augmentation surgery shares many of the same features. She argues that, when enormous breasts are created in a hospital surgery, they are really removing the functionality of the breast tissue, as she notes, rarely is lactational function maintained, and, in any event, it is immaterial to the surgery. The purpose is, as Parker (2009) asserts, a means of meeting the needs of bodily surveillance to which women have been subjected for centuries. They also create a situation where, like with foot binding, movement is made more difficult as enormous breasts make every-day functioning more difficult. Both serve the function of policing the male gaze, how women look to men and how attractive they are, in ways that ignore their needs to be mobile and agile and reduces women's status and function to being desirable to men.

## Social Identity Theory and gendered femininity identity

It is difficult for the authors of this book to understand the need for body modifications. Therefore, in this section of the book, we will provide a number of theories to explain the reasons why foot binding might have been done to young Chinese girls. This is not to justify the act per se but rather to help us understand why such a violent or sexist practice began and why some of these body modifications (e.g., female genital mutilations) may still exists in other parts of the world. Of course, we are unable to cover all these different forms of body modifications in this book, rather we will focus on the practice of foot binding. Many traditional Chinese women believe that bound feet are a sign of wealth and a mean to attract a good marriage for their daughter and/or granddaughter. The bound feet also epitomise Chinese women's beauty, daintiness, and femininity. This gendered ideal and belief is then spread from one generation to the next. Many Chinese women were proud of their bound feet and bound their daughter and/or granddaughter's feet in spite of the pain they knew it caused.

Another way to understand this is through Tajfel's Social Identity Theory (SIT). According to Tajfel (1978), a person's sense of who we are is based on our group membership(s). For many of us, our social class, families or professions are an important source of our pride and self-esteem. In the case of Chinese women who bound their feet, belonging to this group provided them with a superior sense of who they were and where they belonged in China's hierarchical society.

Chinese women have come a long way from the days of bound feet. However, although attempts have been made to stop this cruel practice, foot binding continued in many parts of China even well after its official banning. Simon Montlake (2009) in his article, "Bound by history – The last of China's 'Lotus-Feet' ladies" found that 18% of women in rural Shanxi still had bound feet after 1912. Incredibly, in some remote regions of China such as Yunnan Province, the practice of foot binding continued into the 1950s (Favazza, 2011; Gillet, 2012). According to Ko (2007), the last known case of foot binding was reported in 1957 and the last shoe factory that manufactured lotus shoes closed in Harbin in 1999.

Many Chinese women also grew up with the famous saying from Confucianism, "The virtue of a woman is her lack of knowledge and talent" (Gao, 2003, p. 120). This Confucian ideal has deprived many Chinese women access to any formal education. It was not util 1919 when the first group of Chinese women are allowed to attend Peking National University. This means that many Chinese women do not have access to scientific knowledge and information about their bodies. Nor do they have access to information on how to stop barbaric acts committed to their bodies.

However, Chinese women are not the only group of women who were deprived of formal education. Global statistics show that many women in developing countries such as Afghanistan and India experience differences in mean years of schooling compared to the males in their cultures. Many Muslim women living in these developing countries are also prevented from obtaining formal education. Even if some of them do, they live under constant family, social and cultural scrutiny in a society that does not value education in women.

One of the common factors that all these countries seem to share is that of poverty. Even in developed countries like Australia, poverty has a detrimental impact on women and girls. A case in point is period poverty. Period poverty refers to the inability of some girls to buy sanitary products. A lack of sanitary products leads to a situation of poor health, discomfort and a lower engagement with school affecting girls' educational attainment outcomes (Plan International, 2017; Women's agenda 2020). A survey conducted by Plan International UK (2017) found that one in seven girls (15%) does not have the means to purchase or access of supply to sanitary wear and had to borrow sanitary wear from their friends. Surely, in a wealthy country like Australia, access to menstrual health education and free sanitary products can be made compulsory to increase girls' school attendance, education and ability to find employment.

In doing research for this book, we met several migrant women from poor countries such as Pakistan and India. We became curious about the lives of these migrant women. One of them was Fatimah. Fatimah is from Pakistan and she migrated to Australia with her two children and husband about five years ago. Both Fatimah and her husband are highly educated. Fatimah has a doctoral degree in psychology and her husband has an engineering degree. However, life in Australia has not been easy and despite sending out numerous resumés, Fatimah and her husband are currently working in part-time jobs. Consequently, Fatimah and her family are under constant financial stress. We were able to interview Fatimah about her experiences and what she values in life. (See Box 6.2) below.

---

## BOX 6.2 FATIMAH AND HER MIGRATION EXPERIENCES "DOWN UNDER"

I grew up in a collectivist and patriarchal culture and life has been a roller-coaster ride for me. While my family has been supportive of me in becoming an independent and educated woman, the culture I grew up in has not always been kind to women like myself.

My father is a moderate Muslim who believes that both men and women should have equal access to education. In my family, all my brothers and sisters have attended schools. We are also a very religious family but that has not prevented me from developing a strong cultural and feminine identity.

As a daughter to a moderate Muslim father, I have been fortunate enough to pursue higher study. However, my life changed almost instantly when I got married. My role and identity changed from being a daughter to that of a wife, daughter-in-law, and mother. It has been a struggle to both be a career-minded woman and a wife because working outside the family posed a threat to my husband's masculinity. In fact, my in-laws were unwilling to accept my choice to be a working career woman. Consequently, my mother-in-law cannot understand my choice in wanting to work outside the house.

The situation became stressful when I had children. My husband and I decided that I should work part-time instead of full time to take care of the children. Unfortunately, my husband lost his job and I found myself working part-time to support my family. I remember rushing from my work to pick my children up, cooking dinners, and managing all the housework around the house. I also took care of the social relationships in both my family and my in-law's family. It was a struggle and I found myself always short of time, which made things worse when my home-keeping abilities were criticised by my in-laws. For example, I was criticised for not making home-made meals or cultural foods during one of the social gatherings I had with my in-laws. Eventually, I decided to live for myself and not to worry about other people's judgements. I enrolled as a higher degree student and started

*(Continued)*

conducting research. I was awarded my PhD three years later and decided to migrate to Australia with my husband.

Many things have changed since my migration. I now work at a university and have subsequently become a mentor for my nieces. They have told me that they want to become independent as well rather than depend on their families and/or husbands. This is because many Pakistani men and women believe in a patriarchal status quo that segregate men and women. However, I believe that women in any culture should be able to be educated, to live productive and meaningful lives. This is what I am doing now in Australia.

The good news is that many people around the world believe there is hope for gender parity in terms of access to education. For example, the PEW Research Center conducted a survey in 2019 to see who is getting a good opportunity for education. Most of the people surveyed reported that men and women in their country have approximately the same opportunities to education. Despite this optimism, 1/3 of Turkish respondents and about 1/5 people in Nigeria, Israel, France, Slovakia, Brazil, Japan, and South Korea continued to believe that men have more educational opportunities compared to women. In addition, all countries (except Tunisia) perceived men to still have comparatively more educational opportunities than women, but the great majority believe that opportunities are about equal. So, there is hope for change and hope is a marvellous thing to have.

### First nations women

Australian Indigenous women, like all Indigenous or First Nations people around the world experience higher rates of poverty, unemployment, poor mental and physical health, low educational attainment, racial discrimination, and ongoing marginalisation than other groups (Kendrick, Brooks, Hudson, Thorpe, & Bennett, 2017). Australia has nearly 800,000 Aboriginal and Torres Strait Islander peoples, accounting for approximately 3% of the Australian population (Australian Bureau of Statistics, 2019). Contemporary Aboriginal and Torres Strait Islander peoples are part of the longest continuing culture on earth, with a history that dates back more than 65,000 years. At the time of European colonisation, Australia had an estimated 320,000 Indigenous peoples (Australian Bureau of Statistics, 2002) but colonisation which brought with it "epidemic diseases [that] reduced the population to 80,000" (Smith, 1980). Other practices, including the occupation of land by settlers, the removal of Aboriginal people to 'reserves' and Aboriginal children from their families and land, cultural and domestic abuse, and the loss of language and connection to country further disrupted the experience and lives of Indigenous Australians (Australian Institute of Health and Welfare, 2015, p. 2). Aboriginal and Torres Strait Islander women were among the most affected group.

Indeed, this disruption continues to this day with detrimental impacts to the health and well-being of Indigenous Australians, particularly among Aboriginal and Torres Strait Islander women. For example, compared to non-Indigenous women, Aboriginal and Torres Strait Islander women have higher rates of hospitalisation, physical health issues, mental health issues and mortality as a result of colonisation (Australian Institute of Health and Welfare, 2008, 2015; Australian Health Ministers' Advisory Council, 2006). Aboriginal and Torres Strait Islander women experience assault at a rate 33 times higher than non-Indigenous women (Australian Institute of Health and Welfare, 2008, 2015; Australian Health Ministers' Advisory Council, 2006) and domestic violence rates higher than other women in Australia (Australian Institute of Health and Welfare, 2019), Consequently, Indigenous women are 32 times more likely to be hospitalised and to die from homicide than non-Indigenous women (Better Health, n.d.; Council of Australian Government, 2014).

Aboriginal women also have the largest incarceration rate and are over-represented in the prison system. Approximately one third of female prisoners in New South Wales are Indigenous women (Kendall, Baldry, Sullivan, Sherwood, & Lighton, 2019) despite their low representation in the population. More than 80% of these women are mothers, and the separation from their children combined with being in a prison environment have contributed to high levels of mental health disorders, and the effects resonate through the generations (Kendall, Baldry, Sullivan, Sherwood, & Lighton, 2019). Indigenous children are also significantly over-represented in the Out of Home Care/Foster Care system – they are 10 times more likely than a non-Indigenous child to be in foster care (SBS, 2018).

The gross-over-representation of Aboriginal women in prison, in domestic abuse, poor health, in hospitalisation, and in mortality reflects the inequity, the discrimination, and the failure of multiple agencies to address their needs and concerns. Until there are institutional and systematic changes at both the macro-and micro-levels the negative impact of colonisation on Aboriginal and Torres Strait Islander women will continue and is something that needs to be addressed at many levels, by Governments, advocates, and women generally.

**Trans women and understanding sex and gender diversity**

The T in LGBTIQA+ stands for transgender, but can include trans men and women, or gender non-binary people. Although transgender people in Australia have legal protection, issues of discrimination, or just a lack of understanding, are commonly experienced within society, and there has been calls for cis-gendered women to step up and support the rights of trans people (Kibel, 2021). If you're wondering what cis-gendered means, it is that your gender and sex align – you were born with the sex of a female, for example, and you feel and identify as a female. In other words, the majority of women are cis-gendered (the cis part is pronounced 'sis' in case you weren't sure).

In 2016, Australia's Census asked about sex and gender diversity, with just 1,260 respondents answering they identified as gender diverse. Of course, this number seems considerably lower than the actual proportion of sex and gender diverse people in Australia, however, still provides some insight.

Of the 1,260 respondents to the 2016 Australian Census sex and gender question, 100 were trans female, 70 were trans male, 40 were intersex or indeterminate, 220 were non-binary, 230 were another gender, and 170 were transgender (not otherwise classified). The other 440 respondents did not provide further detail. Within Australia, sex and gender diversity was highest in The Australian Capital Territory (ACT), and the lowest in The Northern Territory (NT). Those reporting sex and gender diversity were far more likely to live in a capital city, compared with regional/rural areas. They were also considerably more likely to have moved location in the year prior to undertaking the Census, indicating possible higher mobility, perhaps due to a younger age profile. Two-thirds (66%) of sex and gender diverse people relocated residence in the previous five years, compared with just 43% of non-sex and gender diverse people. Renting a home was also more likely for sex and gender diverse people (59% rented) compared to the remaining Australian population (31% rented). While this could be due to the age group represented, incomes were generally considerably lower for sex and gender diverse people, on average, at $467 per week, compared to $835 for males, and $536 for females. Despite this, sex and gender diverse people were more likely to complete University studies (37%, compared with 24% of the rest of the population) (ABS, 2018).

To truly embrace diversity, we need to remove an 'us and them' mentality (Kibel, 2021), and accept trans women into women's spaces and conversations. This is the minimum, though, and advocating for those more disadvantaged is an important way of embracing diversity and enabling greater acceptance by others.

## Neurodiversity

In the next section of this chapter, we will be sharing a lived experience of neurodiversity. Heather told us that in Australia not many people know about ASD in females. She wanted to share her story with us because she hopes that more people know more about ASD so that women who suffered ASD can seek the help they need. We post a number of questions to Heather about living with ASD. See box 6.3 below.

**BOX 6.3 HEATHER AND LIVING WITH AUTISM SPECTRUM DISORDER**

Many females with ASD are extremely hyper vigilant socially and emotionally. For many of us, we become obsessed with how we look, what we wear and how we speak. Many of us are literal thinkers. We miss subtle social clues. Our working memory is impaired when we are anxious from the moment we wake up. We make very good eye contact. We enjoy playing games that have rules and purpose. We have a sense of humour. We are kind. We have many interests. We want to achieve and get things right. We work hard to blend in and ultimately to be accepted by the people in the community however, we are completely exhausted and overwhelmed with constant anxiety about the unknown and the possibility of not being accepted because of our awkwardness.

We struggle with the concept of applying moderation in daily life. That may include eating a healthy diet, exercise, healthy thoughts, sex, alcohol, getting out of bed. We can be extreme with interests and become obsessed in the attempt in trying to self-regulate and function on a daily basis. We struggle to navigate the social world. Choosing and maintaining healthy relationships.

My experience was with doctors misdiagnosing me and misrepresenting my needs. I feel like it's dependant on the person seeking help and also on the doctor diagnosing it. Some doctors aren't well educated about what autism is and how it affects people and their daily function. Impaired communication which affects relationships and how we interact with the world. How is someone who is impaired with autism expected to accurately articulate this information with a complete stranger? It's very daunting. It's dependant on their past experience with practitioners and or male or females in the past.

On top of that, there is sensory processing and how we interact with the world. Developmental delays. Plus ADHD.

Our childhood experiences and how we were parented and what we were modelled as children also affects our mindset. We perceive ourselves in a positive or negative way. We have difficulty communicating. Psychiatrists rely on people who can communicate this information to them from the person or the carers. People's values and priorities come into play too. What they consider appropriate or inappropriate, the intensity or repetition, or intensity of a habit isn't shared.

My experience with doctors/psychiatrists was that they are like builders looking for a contract on their books for the next 12 months. Clients to fill for private hospital bed, daily visits in the ward while they change medication for the next six weeks. They seem to line their

(Continued)

pockets so they can afford their $700,000 mortgage and their Audi 7. They aren't really interested in you or your problems.

For women with ASD, I recommend that they see a developmental paediatrician and have access to the NDIS with providers such as occupational therapist, speech pathologist, psychologist, physiotherapist, educational literacy specialist who educate the person, and the family that provide skills and understanding. They are important because these are people who can advocate for women suffering from ASD.

I have found that women with ASD are often misdiagnosed with bipolar by psychiatrists who would write a script for a bottle or 4 bottles of drugs and tell us that we have ADHD, depression, anxiety and OCD and must have regular stays at their private hospital. The drugs dull the big feeling so you feel empty. It's easy to give someone a script and say come back and see me every week or every fortnight. These drugs may work they may not. Let's trial them!

Some psychiatrists will tell us to let's try group sessions with other men and women who have bipolar and do cognitive behaviour therapy. These group sessions may be useful for people with addictions such as eating disorders, drugs, sex, dangerous adrenaline seeking behaviour, alcohol addictions, but they are not useful for us who have a communication impairment.

I feel we need to do so much more for women with ASD and I hope my story can be a beacon for them. We need to learn how to manage these women's needs, and to respond to their cues so we can understand why we don't respond to yours. It's also important employers see us as valuable, as special and as having many gifts that can be useful in an organisation, rather than misunderstand us and think we are being standoffish or rude.

## Looking to the future

This chapter focused on some of the diverse lives of women in contemporary society and cultures. The chapter may have started with Chinese women's three-inch bound feet and how those bound feet served to restrict their body, their mind as well as their social freedom. What we also found was that women from other cultures, societies, and backgrounds were also bound by different forms of traumas or experiences in their lives. Some of the contributory factors to these traumas may be the old-fashioned ways of doing things, the lack of formal education, poverty, institutional discrimination, abuse, or misdiagnosis. Nevertheless, women have made significant advances in the past 25 years, especially in the area of formal education. UNESCO, for example, is leading and coordinating the Education 2030 Agenda. Its aim is to focus on a system-wide transformation including providing data that puts gender equality into action in and through education, and better legal, policy, and planning frameworks (UNESCO, 2019). We also know that the discrepancy in educational attainment between men and women has narrowed significantly. However, there are still areas such as family laws, medical knowledge, and welfare that as a society we need to continue to advocate so that vulnerable women can also live productive and happy lives.

## Reference list

Australian Bureau of Statistics (2002). Year book, Australia, 2002. ABS cat. no. 1301.0. Canberra: ABS.

Australian Bureau of Statistics (2018). Sex and gender diversity: Characteristics of the responding population. Retrieved from https://www.abs.gov.au/ausstats/abs@. nsf/Lookup/by%20Subject/2071.0~2016~Main%20Features~Sex%20and%20 Gender%20Diversity:%20Characteristics%20of%20the%20Responding%20 Population~103.

Australian Bureau of Statistics (2019). Estimates and projections, Aboriginal and Torres Strait Islander Australians, 2006 to 2031. ABS cat. no. 3238.0. Canberra: ABS.

Australian Health Ministers' Advisory Council (2006). Aboriginal and Torres Strait Islander health performance framework report 2006. Canberra: AHMAC.

Australian Institute of Health and Welfare (2008). The health and welfare of Australia's Aboriginal and Torres Strait Islander Peoples. AIHW cat. no. IHW 21; ABS cat. no. 4704.0.

Australian Institute of Health and Welfare (2015). The health and welfare of Australia's Aboriginal and Torres Strait Islander peoples. Retrieved from https:// www.aihw.gov.au/getmedia/584073f7-041e-4818-9419-39f5a060b1aa/18175.pdf. aspx?inline=true.

Australian Institute of Health and Welfare (2019). Family, domestic and sexual violence in Australia: Continuing the national story 2019. Cat. no. FDV 3. Canberra: AIHW.

Better Health (n.d.). Family violence and Aboriginal and Torres Strait Islander women. Retrieved from https://www.betterhealth.vic.gov.au/health/healthyliving/ Family-violence-and-aboriginal-and-torres-strait-islander-women.

Blake, F. (1994). Foot-binding in neo-Confucian China and the appropriation of female labor. *Signs, 19*(3), 676–712. doi:10.1086/494917.

Council of Australian Government (2014). The national plan to reduce violence against women and their children 2010–2022. Retrieved from https://www.dss. gov.au/sites/default/files/documents/08_2014/national_plan1.pdf.

Dettwyler, K.A. (1995). Beauty and the breast: The cultural context of feeding in the United States. In S. Macadam. & K.A. Dettwyler (Eds.), *Breastfeeding: Biocultural perspectives* (pp. 167–215). New York: Aldine de Gruyter.

Favazza, A. (2011). *Bodies under siege: Self-mutilation, non-suicidal self-injury, and body modification in culture and psychiatry*, 3rd ed. Baltimore, MD: John Hopkins University Press.

Gao, X. Y. (2003). Women existing for men: Confucianism and social injustice against women in China. *Race, Gender & Class, 10*(3), 114–125.

Gillet, K. (2012, April). In China, foot binding slowly slips into history. *Los Angeles Times*. Retrieved from https://www.latimes.com/world/la-xpm-2012-apr-16-la-fg-china-bound-feet-20120416-story.html.

Hong, F. (1997). *Foot-binding, feminism and freedom: The liberation of women's bodies in m modern China.* London: Routledge.

Kendall, S., Baldry, E., Sullivan, E., Sherwood, J., & Lighton, S. (2019). Aboriginal mothers are incarcerated at alarming rates – and their mental and physical health suffers. Retrieved from https://theconversation.com/aboriginal-mothers-are-incarcerated-at-alarming-rates-and-their-mental-and-physical-health-suffers-116827

Kendrick, J., Brooks, R., Hudson, J., Thorpe, M., & Bennett, P. (2017). Aboriginal and Torres Strait Islander healing programs: A literature review. Retrieved from https://healingfoundation.org.au/app/uploads/2017/02/Aboriginal-and-Torres-Strait-Islander-Healing-Programs-A-Literature-Review.pdf.

Kibel (2021, February). It's time cisgender women did more to protect the rights of transgender Australians. Retrieved from https://fashionjournal.com.au/life/cisgender-women-transgender-people/.

Ko, D. (2007). *Cinderella's sisters: A revisionist history of foot-binding.* Los Angeles: University of California Press.

Mao, J. (2007). Foot binding: Beauty and torture. *The Internet Journal of Biological Anthropology, 1*(2), 8–8. Miltner, L. J. (1937). Bound feet in China. *The Journal of Bone and Joint Surgery, 19*(2), 314–319.

Montlake, S. (2009, November 13). Bound by history: The last of China's 'Lotus-Feet' ladies. *Wall Street Journal.* Retrieved from https://www.wsj.com/articles/SB125800116737444883.

O'Toole, L. L., & Schiffman, J. R. (1997). *Gender violence: Interdisciplinary perspectives.* New York: New York University Press.

Parker, R. (2009). The female body and body image: A historical perspective. In *Women, doctors and cosmetic surgery* (pp. 25–37). London: Palgrave Macmillan.

Plan International UK (2017). 1 in 10 girls have been unable to afford sanitary wear, survey finds. Retrieved from https://plan-uk.org/media-centre/1-in-10-girls-have-been-unable-to-afford-sanitary-wear-survey-finds.

Renzetti, C. M. et al. (2008, 6 August). *Encyclopaedia of interpersonal violence. 1.* Los Angeles, CA: SAGE Publications.

SBS (2018). Indigenous children 10 times more likely to be placed in foster care. Retrieved from https://www.sbs.com.au/nitv/nitv-news/article/2018/11/27/indigenous-children-10-times-more-likely-be-placed-foster-care.

Smith, L. R. (1980). *The Aboriginal population of Australia.* Canberra: Australian National University Press.

Stewart, M. W. (2014). *Ordinary violence: Everyday assaults against women worldwide,* 2nd ed. Santa Barbara, CA: Praeger.

Tajfel, H. (1978). Differentiation between social groups: Studies in the social psychology of intergroup relations. London: Academic Press.

UNESCO (2019). From access to empowerment UNESCO strategy for gender equality in and through education 2019–2025. Retrieved from https://unesdoc.unesco.org/ark:/48223/pf0000369000.

Women's Agenda (2020). New study uncovers reality of period poverty in Australian schools. Retrieved from https://womensagenda.com.au/latest/new-study-uncovers-reality-of-period-poverty-in-australian-schools/#:~:text=Period%20poverty%20is%20the%20term, with%20school%20and%20community%20activities.

# 7 The contemporary landscape for women

Less mental clutter means more mental resources available for deep thinking.
—Cal Newport, Deep Work: Rules for Focused Success
in a Distracted World

## A story about the COVID lockdown and how little men stepped up

When the COVID-19 pandemic happened in 2020, the lockdown further exacerbated the inequalities in many heterosexual relationships. Not only were women losing their jobs more than men (Hinsliff, 2020), those that kept their jobs were finding they were doing not only more work at home (Butler, 2020) but also more of the housework and more of the home-learning that came along with the kids not going to school (Summers, 2020). These women were stretched to the limit and were probably just trying to do anything effectively, let alone do everything.

Statistics were revealing here, the impact on women's careers was massive and the effects lasted long after the lockdown ended and when masks as personal accessory became a "remember when we had to wear masks?" meme. Mothers were more likely to have quit or been furloughed or made redundant at one and a half times the rate of men (Todd, 2021). They were also much more likely to combine paid work with other activities and do more of the unpaid labour of childcare than their male partners. Even though men involved themselves more in childcare, and did some housework, during the lockdown (Schulte & Swenson, 2020), it was not at the same rate as women who picked up most of the burden of care. This was particularly the case for mothers, as children were kept home from school and women tended to support most of the schooling work done at home. Mothers were also more likely to be interrupted by the kids and still carried the bulk of the housework load, in addition to putting food on the table, compared to fathers (Charlton, 2020).

Was anyone surprised? It was always known that women in heterosexual relationships did more work around the house than men (Charlton, 2020),

DOI: 10.4324/9781003020554-8

that work included all those unpaid, but vital, jobs. From cleaning the toilet to collecting the kids from school when they were sick, it was women's work to do these chores that were vital but under-resourced and under-valued because they were unpaid.

These issues for women came on the back of mental health statistics that revealed there was a mental health gap between men and women which was exacerbated by the lockdown (Charlton, 2020). Beyond this, sadly, expected findings around intimate partner violence and anxiety and the rate of job losses, studies conducted in the USA during lockdown revealed mental health issues increased for women while not budging a statistically significant amount for men (Charlton, 2020). Women, who took on more of the house duties, the childcare, the children's education and the stress of losing their jobs at a greater rate, generally had a decline in their mental health that exacerbated already existing differences between men and women's mental health (Charlton, 2020). Girls can do anything, but it can come at a cost to their mental health or well-being.

These issues are also not new. In the late 1980s, Dr Marilyn Waring wrote a book called 'If Women Counted'. This book argued that many of the current and popular economics policies were wrong because they didn't consider the unpaid work of women in the nation's GDP (Waring, 1989). She argued for a feminist economics in which we rebalanced the effects of work on people's lives, both the paid work we do for employers and the unpaid work we, mostly women, do to keep the world running. She said the current economic system was out of whack because it counted among GDP the environmental disasters of oil spills and war but did not count the work of women in the home, in childrearing, in education, in caring and in keeping the house working (Waring, 1989). Underpinning all economics, Waring argued, is the unpaid work mostly women do in the home to allow for other economic activities to proceed (Waring, 1989). If we were all sick because the toilet was unclean or the benches had bacteria or there was no soap in the shower, it would be pretty difficult to do the work we all do for our employer.

These issues are at the forefront of how we manage the world of work today. And, they played in to the issues faced by women during the 2020 COVID-19 lockdown. While many women resented the role they had to play, such as the increased caring responsibilities and overseeing the school at home for children, in many households, it was not questioned that it would fall to women. Of course, women would have to step up, the work they did became an extension to the work they did in normal times. It exacerbated their workloads, and many men realised how much was involved in the work women did, but it still didn't change. It's nice to get honours and to be thanked, but help would go a lot further towards women experiencing a break than simply hearing, "good on you, hon".

Other issues that came from this period were the revealing of other cracks in the system that keeps women in employment. These cracks are generally around childcare. Childcare is a contentious issue in many countries. And, much like the work women do at home, the impact of a disrupted or unreliable or expensive child care system falls disproportionately to women, even though childcare should be a family issue, not an issue for women. It is, in many cases, women whose work suffers if she can't get the children in to care, it is women whose career suffers when she has to take time off for caring responsibilities and it is women who bear the brunt of having to step up and do the childcare if the system fails the family (Charlton, 2020). Of course, this is not the case in all family situations, but it is a more common scenario than the reverse.

Care work also impacts on time. Research (for example, Burkeman, 2018) suggests that, just because you get a job as a woman, and that's not just a woman with a middle-class job in the first world it's all women, any woman in any part of the world loses time. What that means is that women, regardless of where they live, do a little less caring when they do paid work but that does not mean they do less of the caring overall, and that when they get a job, they do much more work than men.

And, yes, there are exceptions to the rule. There are men who do more work than women in the home. There are men who quit their jobs and do the full-time care of very young children just after birth. There are men who do their share of the house and caring work in the home. There are men who take time off work when their child is unwell or has appointments. However, on balance, the bulk of the responsibilities for childcare, for housework and for any other kind of unpaid labour falls disproportionately to women even as they have increased their hours at paid work over the years. Girls can do everything indeed, and it seems that, even when she is doing the paid work she is qualified for, or that keeps the family's finances solvent, she is still doing the other stuff that keeps the family alive and well.

In this chapter, we will look at some of these issues. We'll look at time management, what we know from the academic research into time management in workplaces, how are different women's times managed, what works and what doesn't? We will also look at how the time is managed in relation to the issues that women face in managing the work/life balance. The next section is looking at keeping all the balls in the air. How women juggle it all, and make the world keep turning for everyone. The third section is about demystifying the ways women's work is impacted by children, the 'mothering for schooling' work women are in engaged in the ways that women assist children to be successful in their schooling careers. Finally, the last section deals with the politics of relationships and how couples, and single mothers, manage their children's needs, their employer's/employers' needs, and keep the house going.

## Time management: a new surveillance environment what do we know, how do we work best?

During the COVID lockdown, many employers allowed staff to work off site, where work could be conducted at home. Of those, some employed new software to surveil staff. Normally, surveillance happens in a physical space. In middle class jobs, it's the line manager walking around and checking we aren't just internet shopping while we are supposed to be working or posting on our TikTok while we are on a client call or gossiping about the staff member speaking to a friend on text while we are trapped in a meeting room. Or maybe you even text fellow colleagues in meetings saying, "that should have been an email"?

Several tools were implemented in middle-class (office) jobs during lockdowns that policed the work an employee was doing. There were questions around both their efficacy and their morality. Most of the tools were a program that ran in the background either with or without the employee's active participation. Some of them were run in the background and generated a report on the progress of the employee to both the line manager and to the employee themselves. They were quite crude and very quantitative, they measure amount of time on different sites, amount of time on different programs, number of emails sent, number of calls made, and number of responses the employee makes. Some companies beefed these tools up with frequent check ins from management. However, academic research (Blumenfeld, Anderson & Hooper, 2020) suggests this approach is not only overkill, it's also ineffective. Employees who can work from home tend to be more efficient and tend to be able to manage their time when they have tasks to complete and are able to complete them. These findings hold doubly true for women.

We have already established women do more than their fair share of the caring work, so how can working from home and flexible schedules help women? When working from home, women can arrange their workday so that they can meet the needs of their children. They can also be there to do school pick-up and drop-off without having to get themselves ready for going into the office. There is also evidence that women are responsibilised to work hard, and that all employees, not just women, do more work when they are in a flexible setting. The example in Box 7.1 shows how Catherine tries to juggle everything in her life.

---

**BOX 7.1  CATHERINE'S STORY: JUGGLING AND HOW TO KEEP ALL THE BALLS IN THE AIR**

Catherine has two children, one on the Autism Spectrum (ASD) who also presents with Attention-Deficit/Hyperactivity Disorder (ADHD) and another, neurotypical child. The two children, boys, are aged six and four. Catherine has been a single mum who now lives with her partner who suffers from depression. However, he is not the father of the children. She runs the household completely, tries to carry the mental load of a partner suffering depression, while simultaneously preparing herself for work and her children for school. Both the boys are at school, but due to various issues they present, they're with her a lot more than they should be. Nothing changed for her during the COVID lockdown, it was more of the same. However, some of it was a relief, her ASD son had fewer meltdowns and she was able to do a bit of sewing. Catherine puts extreme pressure on herself to achieve in all aspects of her life but finds she has little time for the things she loves, including exercise (yoga) and sewing.

As a single mum, her partner sometimes does some washing or some childcare, but most of that work falls to her and she is constantly exhausted at the end of the day. She tries to restrict screen time, but that just puts more work on her as she's called on to play more actively with the children.

Work is a break from the intensity of her home life and the staff in her staff room at her teaching job provide a relief from the daily grind, adult conversation, and also some information on her son's condition. She is somewhat supported from an organisational perspective at her work, but she puts a lot of pressure on herself to be everything to everyone.

Catherine sometimes has moments when she feels like she is "winning" at work or parenting, though she feels like she is constantly learning in both parenting home life and also work life. She feels like an amateur in both work and home/parenting. The latter is especially hard, even when she tries to do some yoga, however it's hard attempting to practice when she's over-run with children climbing over her and demanding things. Time management is non-existent, she says her life is a, "a shit roller coaster" when she's solo parenting a child on the Autism Spectrum and ADHD and a four year old. The magic time tricks may exist, but they're a pipe dream in her current situation. All she wants is some kind of balance and a chance to go to the toilet by herself.

What can we see from Catherine's story? We can see how hard it is to do all the work that parents have to do. We can see how important employee supports are to helping women who are in Catherine's position manage their load. We can also see how important the job is to Catherine's well-being and mental health. Catherine said she needs to have a word with her partner, to ask him to do more around the house. She has also accessed government services to get help for her sons, particularly the one with special needs. She's also trying to leave her son with special needs with her partner more to spend some quality one-on-one time with her other son. When we spoke with her after the interview, she said just talking to us made her see the situation more clearly. She recommended journaling as a strategy that was working for her and preventing her from letting frustrations build so she could see the situation in black and white before her, rather than it being more abstracted as she just drifted through her days.

## Dads don't babysit

'Women's work' is an expression in research into families and parenting. We're not talking about paid employment when we discuss 'women's work'. That's just work. 'Women's work' is the work that is pretty much always unpaid, around the house, it's gendered female but, without it, the world just wouldn't work. An example is childcare. In two parent, heterosexual families, the work of managing children's tasks usually falls to women. It's things like what mothers do to get their children school ready (teaching early phonemic awareness and taking them to music, Gymboree and other activities), the work they do on homework, the work they do to manage their children's outside of school activities, the management of child care, of choosing schools, of choosing outside activities, and usually getting them there, the help they give their children with their friends, their social relationships, their familial obligations to others in the family, their housework, and, after that, their jobs (i.e., their paid work). They may have time to go to the bathroom by themselves but, as Catherine's vignette points out, that's more often than not a pipe dream.

Annette Lareau talked in her famous book, 'Home Advantage', of the work mothers do to prepare their children for, and manage, their schooling. This work is gendered, in the sense that it's usually mothers who do this stuff, and classed, in the sense that different social classes see the work of raising their children differently. Middle-class parents tend to see themselves as part of the teaching relationship with their children and their children's teachers. The teacher does the work in the school and the mother does the work in the home such as homework, reading to their children, listening to them read, talking about the school day and the learning that occurred and being up front at the school when there were issues. We all remember those mums who turned up at the school because their child had experienced some injustice and how the teachers, and the admin staff, quaked at their presence. One of our authors remembers a mother who made the school pulp all the booklets for an orchestral performance (all 1,000 of them) because they'd misspelled her daughter's last name. By contrast, working class parents saw their children's teachers in the same way you might see a surgeon, they're interested in what's going on, but school was strictly teachers' domain. This same author remembers the jealousy at this girl's mother when her own mother's response to every thing that was reported happing at school was, "my goodness me, you tell such awful lies about your teachers!".

The difference in mothering approaches impacts everything, but especially homework. Lareau talked about how middle-class parents saw the home as an extension of the child's place of work, the school, where homework and extra learning might occur while the working-class parent saw the home as separated from the school and didn't see school in terms of a workplace. In these terms, the middle-class parents took on more of the responsibility for teaching and learning than the working-class parents and this difference impacted the child's experiences in school. Children's success was highly correlated with their parents' social class position. All parents had high hopes for their children, it's just that middle class parents had a better idea of how to make that success happen, and worked with their children in different ways, to ensure it happened.

Building on this work was the work of Griffith and Smith (2004) in Australia. They looked at who in the family does the work to make sure children are successful at school. They found it was generally mothers do the work, in heterosexual families, to make sure children are successful in school (academically and socially). This work isn't just remembering to pack a sports kit on a Thursday evening for Friday's sports class, it's also remembering who has violin and when and who has a friend whose party is Saturday week and what on earth this child likes so we can get them a great present. Basically, Griffith and Smith (2004) argue it's mothers (in heterosexual families) who did this extra stuff with their children to ensure they were successful in school. Mothers did the schlepping around, the homework, listening to infinite readers and police the assignments and got costumes and posters and all the things required to ensure that child was successful. This extra activity comes at no small cost to mothers in heterosexual, partnered relationships. It comes at even greater cost to mothers who are not partnered. The authors of this book have observed, however, that with traditional schooling, tasks seem to increasingly shared between men and women – from school drop offs and pick-ups, to parent/teacher meeting nights. Often Mum might do the school drop off, and Dad will do the school pick up, or they'll take it in turns to handle science nights and interviews with the teachers. When it comes to volunteers at the school breakfasts, or the canteen, though, or even P&C committees, far more women do seem to step up than men. And the research shows that women are doing more of the school support work at home.

All this work places a huge additional burden on mothers to do more work once the children come along. There is evidence that, in partnered, heterosexual families, men's time spent on parenting has increased since the 1980s when many children were being parented by dads who didn't ever know our friends' names (all the authors have horror stories of our dads forgetting various friends' names), even though they turned up at our house every weekend. Evidence suggests between 1965 and 2011 dads' share of the childcare workload in the average American family increased by 2.5 hours per week. It's a snail's pace, but it is a move in the right direction. However, over that same time period, women's share of the childcare workload has increased from 10 to 14 hours per week. The gap's getting smaller, but it's still there. Research finds that the birth of a child increases mum's workload by 21 hours per week and dad's workload increases by 12.5 hours, a 70% difference in total workload for women than men (Charlton, 2020). These hours add up and make a difference over years so that women are doing paid work and childcare at a rate not seen in men. Ultimately this can impact on career progression, or simply result in women trying to do it all. Women do more of the housework, more of the childcare and more of the management of schedules and more of the nursing a child who's ill. In other words, they do more work that is directly related to the management of the children (Charlton, 2020). While all of this is occurring, women are doing more leadership roles at work, and are more likely to work full time than ever before (Australian Institute of Family Studies, 2021). Is it any wonder women are, more often than not, responding with 'busy' when asked how they are?

Research also suggests, in two parent, heterosexual families, mum might be more reluctant to give up some of the work to dad. Partly due to the belief that women should be able to cope, partly due to the belief that it's women's work, a persistent but still strong stereotype, and partly due to a sense that they should be able to do anything or everything, women tend to take on more of the responsibility and seem reluctant to give some of it up.

## All the single ladies and same sex relationships

Sometimes, we read stories about women struggling to find a man (Tong, 2019) or, as it's colloquially known, the 'man drought'. While many heterosexual women choose to not have a relationship, for others, it's less about choice and more about not finding the right person. A firm that focuses on trends developed a beautiful graphic of what they termed the 'man drought' in 2018 to describe the states, and even the suburbs, with the fewest men. Their information suggests there were around 100,000 more women than men in Australia, with six out of eight states and territories having more women than men.

Perhaps this explains why, on average, we are getting married later than we did in the 1970s (AIFS, 2021)? The crude marriage rate, that's the rate of marriages per 1,000 population, was 5.5 in 2009 down from 6 in 1999 (ABS, 2020). While smaller numbers of people are getting married, we are also getting married later. In 1999, the median age was 27.9 years while, in 2019, it was 30.5 (ABS, 2020). These statistics suggest we are either experiencing a man drought, which the demographic firms and media want us to think, or there are a confluence of factors and man-droughts may be only one of those factors. Interestingly, couples divorce less than they used to, with the crude divorce rate down between 1999, when 2.8 divorces per 1,000 persons were granted a divorce compared with 2019 when the crude divorce rate was 1.9 per 1,000 persons.

Same sex marriages, for obvious reasons, were higher in 2018 than in previous years. Same-sex marriage was legalised in 2017 (AG, 2018). In 2018, there were 6,538 same-sex marriages but that number dropped to 5,507 in 2019, potentially as the initial rush of legal marriages went through (ABS, 2020). We have talked a bit about same-sex marriages in the previous section, but below (See Box 7.2), let's hear a bit more about their decision to get married…. Or not.

---

**BOX 7.2 MARRIAGE DECISIONS FOR TWO COUPLES –
ALEX & CASSANDRA AND JADE & SARAH**

Alex and Cassandra had been together for over ten years when same-sex marriage became legalised. They had a commitment ceremony after they had been together four years. Their friend, Jade, was one of the attendants at their wedding. Jade had been in short term relationships, or single, for most of Alex and Cassandra's relationship, but in 2014 met Sarah and settled down quickly.

Once the decision around legalising same-sex marriage was made, the two couples went out for dinner together. Jade and Sarah were excitedly sharing that they had planned to get married – they couldn't wait to tie the knot, and expected Alex and Cassandra felt the same way. Alex and Cassandra were thrilled that same-sex marriage had now become legal – it meant a lot to them, but they didn't really feel the desire to legally marry. "We had a big wedding already", Cassandra said, referring to their commitment ceremony, "and I'm not sure if we want to take the magic away from that day by getting married". Over the coming year, Jade and Sarah planned their wedding, and Alex and Cassandra were attendants, but it still didn't create the need in them in legally marry. Over the coming years, Alex and Cassandra saw couples make different decisions. Some who had had commitment ceremonies married legally, some opted not to, and some had no interest in any formalised lifelong commitment, legal or not. But all were happy that same sex marriage had been legalised, giving couples the choice.

---

When women get married, if they decide to have children, they have another choice to make, what to do about going back to work when they become mothers. Most Australian women go back to work after the baby is born (Australian Institute of Family Studies, 2021), but there are more women who choose not to go back to work, for myriad reasons. In the next section, we consider the issues faced by this group of women.

## Stay at home mums

There are some women who choose to opt out when they have children. They decide that the race, the stress, the trying to have it all is too much to bear and they'd rather not live their lives constantly rushing. Or maybe, once they met that little person in the delivery room, they didn't want to do anything except be with them. Or, is it more complex? Here is Katie's story (see Box 7.3 below).

## BOX 7.3 KATIE'S STORY – BEING A STAY-AT-HOME MUM

Katie was 24 when she fell pregnant with her first, a boy. Being from a large family, she had always been around lots of children. She'd had a professional job, Katie worked as a marketing assistant, before she fell pregnant and worked throughout the pregnancy. She had assumed she would want to go back to work after he was born. However, when she met Ryden, she knew she couldn't leave him to someone else to care for. Family helped, and she had her mum and her husband's mum and her sisters to help out, but she still didn't feel comfortable leaving him. There was also the issue of money. George, Katie's husband, earned a lot more than Katie. Even with the help of family, she realised she would have to leave Ryden with carers outside the family for two or three days a week. If she went part time, the effort she would need to go to didn't seem economically viable either. So, Katie became a stay-at-home mum.

She had another three children – another boy called Jayden, a girl called Kate-Lynn and her youngest was a boy called Mason. Katie knew she couldn't manage working and being the kind of mum her children needed, so, she and George made sacrifices. They didn't update their car, they didn't wear the most expensive clothes or the best shoes. They bought on sale. They shopped at Costco and Aldi, rather than at the brand name shops or at markets. They got by.

When asked why she had stayed at home, Katie said it was a few factors. At first, she would tell people it was the economics of it, it made better economic sense for her to stay home. But, if she told the truth, it was more about her need to be with her children. Her choice to be there. She wanted to be there for them before they went to school. She wanted to be at the pick-up after school finished every day. She wanted to attend sports carnivals, volunteer in the classroom and at the tuckshop. She wanted to be there if her kids were sick at school to take them straight home.

As early as 2018, Forbes magazine (Lundram, 2018) was reporting that the biggest rise in stay-at-home mums (SAHMs for short) was amongst millennials. The Pew Research Centre describes this generation as the most educated, the most empowered, and the most indebted generation (Bialik & Fry, 2019) but also the group most likely to report staying home after having children and not returning to work. While their older sisters in Gen X and their Boomer mothers had forged a path to working motherhood, the millennial generation had decided that path was not for all of them. Some were happier at home, happier with a more traditionally sanctioned pathway for their families, one where their partner went to work and they stayed home.

It is worth noting, this group is not the majority, not by a long shot. With mortgages through the roof (which, if you struggle to afford the mortgage, fixing the roof is just another astronomical expense you do not need) and living expenses that are eye-watering, it's surprising that, in spite of all their education and their expenses, and the social sanctions that come from being a SAHM (Bodiat, 2020), the Australian Bureau of Statistics in Australia (Australian institute of Family Studies, 2021) reported 27% of mothers in 2016 chose to stay at home, not much of a change on the 33% who chose to stay at home in 1991 when the millennials were the babies, and it was their mother who was staying home. But, what about all the opportunities young women have had? The fight to keep that job long after they'd had their babies, a fight our mothers had to fight?

US research suggests that there has been a slowdown in the gender revolution (Budge & Charles, 2020). Far from liberalising the attitudes to gender and work and women's lives, since the year 2000, these attitudes have actually become more traditional. As such, they report that the difficulties in combining both work and family responsibilities, particularly in the USA, as well as social forces that maintain gender gaps and privilege time intensive mother practices are also changing. So, is Katie that unusual in the post-2000s climate?

Katie makes an allusion to the mothering practices that favour intensive parenting in her story. She says she felt she couldn't return to work after giving birth to Ryden, as she wouldn't be able to be the kind of mum he needed after she'd given herself to others for a day at work. She also suggested that she didn't feel she could let strangers raise her kids, and that school was close enough to that for her. Her attitude is not unusual in the millennial cohort. Hays (1996) describes how millennials see giving everything up for their children as the very epitome of "good mothering", O'Riley (2019) calls it "patriarchal mothering" and Douglas and Michels (2005) call it "the new momism". It is characterised by an overwhelming need to give everything to a child, to put yourself and your needs after that of your children (but the same need does not extend to your male partner or other non-mothering adults in the child's life). It leads to a situation where the mother may lose the other parts of her identity not related to her reproductive practices and where mothering becomes the most important thing a woman does, regardless of what she may have done as an individual prior to children, or what she'll do after her kids have left. As Hallstein (2017) states, this practice of "institutionalized motherhood today simultaneously acknowledges the large-scale changes brought about by second wave feminisms, while also being a backlash ideology that keeps mothers primarily responsible, still, for childrearing and family-life management".

For many of these women, the intention was to stay at home while their children were young and to go back to work when they were established at school (Gale, 2017), and they were not SAHMs. However, in the USA at least, the Pew Research Centre (Cohn & Caumont, 2017) suggests they are more likely to be religious, and have lower rates of education, which means they are less able to find work, than women who go back to work after children. The majority of SAHMs still choose to stay home, rather than doing so out of necessity – Pew Research Centre data suggests that only 6% are at home because they can't find work. For many it can be an attractive choice – other than having more time with their children, stay at home mothers, on average, reportedly get more sleep and leisure time than their working counterparts. There is also a belief among some millennial women that there is more to life than being grist to a capitalist mill than their Boomer mothers or their Gen X sisters may believe (Cook, 2018). For many, it's described as a feminist choice, one that is about having the opportunities to do what you want, what you think is right, in spite of what may be considered to be societal expectations that you'd want to have it all.

### The ageing trap: no (more) kids but your parents are now on your hands? Or maybe you're just a Club Sandwich!

Not long after our children have left, or as our children are needing us less and less, some women find themselves in the position of needing to look after our parents. These women are considered part of the 'Sandwich Generation', looking after both your own children and your parents at the same time (or, as a colleague suggested, she's a 'Club Sandwich', looking after her mother, her young adult children as they get their lives in order, and her grandchildren!).

In 2019, the NY Times asked where all the working women were, and they answered, they were at their parents' houses, again, but this time, they were doing the caring (Porter, 2019, August 29). In the USA, this phenomenon is termed a crisis in caregiving as adult women gave up what is sometimes the most economically productive time in their lives to care for older relatives. A report from the USA found that more than a quarter of respondents had been warned by their employers that they were jeopardising their employment by caring for older relatives (Home Instead, 2019). They also found that around 40% of respondents reported being passed over for promotion or a pay rise and they stated they had the quality of their work suffer because they were doing caring work for older relatives, usually parents. The same story happens in Australia too. In Australia, an organisation called Your Side, an aged care provider in Sydney who provides home care and National Disability Insurance Scheme (NDIS) packages to older Sydneysiders, called for carers of ageing and infirm family members to be offered a type of leave similar to paid parental and sick leave (Women's Agenda, 2019). An article about carers in Australia found that 57% of carers were women, mostly aged over 45 (Women's Agenda, 2019). These women, all 2.65 million of them, provided informal care to ageing and infirm relatives aged over 65 (Women's Agenda, 2019). These women find their career trajectory affected, and their workforce engagement negatively impacted, when they undertake this type of caring responsibility (Women's Agenda, 2019). In addition, as Annabel Crabb (2019) noted, it is often on top of having taken time out to raise their own children and now they're back to do it all again with their parents. Nola's story is similar (see Box 7.4 below).

Women need support while they are undertaking caring responsibilities. The work of caring for older relatives tends to fall to women (Power, 2020). They also need access to high level supports for their financial, emotional,

---

**BOX 7.4 NOLA'S STORY**

Nola planned to get straight back into the workforce when her children were old enough. When her youngest got to high school and didn't need his mum so much, she thought things were going to be great. But then things started to go badly for her parents. First, her dad had a fall. He was fine, at first, but it was clear it had affected him deeply. He didn't trust himself anymore and began relying more and more on Nola's mum. Then, he had a series of heart attacks. Nola's mum and dad lived in another city, about 45 minutes' drive from Nola, but she made the journey weekly, then every other day, to check on them both as they became weaker and more obviously in need of care. Nola was trying to manage this after a day of work, she worked as an advertising copywriter for a local newspaper. She began to notice her dad was forgetting things. He would pop the kettle on but then forget to turn it off as it sang loudly from the kitchen.

One day, when Nola was at work, the fire brigade called because he had started a fire in the kitchen. It was obvious, to everyone who knew him, that he was increasingly needing a more intense form of care. Nola's mum was loath to put him into a home, but it became obvious he would need more help than she could provide and Nola was struggling. The newspaper, like many regional papers, eventually folded but that meant that there was nothing stopping Nola from taking on all the caring work. While she did not mind taking care of her parents and was finding balancing her day job with her caring responsibilities overwhelming, working at the newspaper was her love, she did not want to give it up. Her father lived in the home for about 18 months, but shortly after, her mother had a fall and broke her hip. She too was put into a home. After her mother died, Nola realised she spent almost seven years progressively increasing her caring responsibilities with her parents which, while it didn't cost her the job she loved, interfered with her capacity to be herself, outside of caring and meant that, after her parents' deaths, she struggled to find more work.

and physical well-being when they take up caring responsibilities for older relatives (Singleton, 2000). Nola's story is not unusual, it is often the case that women have children at home while also caring for older relatives (Manor, 2021). The article in Women's Agenda argues for a carers' leave package for (mostly) women caring for their relatives, if we can provide flexible work and leave arrangements for women who are caring for young children, why can't we do the same for women caring for adult relations? And, this package should be extended to our sisters in gig work and on casual contracts. All women deserve the dignity of making choices that work for them and if they choose to care for older relations, the whole community benefits, but nobody should be worse off economically if they carry the hard work, and the emotional load, of caring in the middle and later stages of their careers.

### Reference list

ABS (Australian Bureau of Statistics) (2020). Marriages and divorces, Australia. Retrieved from https://www.abs.gov.au/statistics/people/people-and-communities/marriages-and-divorces-australia/latest-release.

AG (Attorney-General's Department). Marriage equality: Questions and answers on sex and gender. Retrieved from https://www.ag.gov.au/sites/default/files/2020-03/marriage-equality-faq.pdf.

Australian Institute of Family Studies (2021). Marriage rates in Australia. Retrieved from https://aifs.gov.au/facts-and-figures/marriage-rates-australia.

Bialik, K., & Fry, R. (2019, January 30). Millenial life: How young adulthood today compares with prior generations. Retrieved from https://www.pewresearch.org/social-trends/2019/02/14/millennial-life-how-young-adulthood-today-compares-with-prior-generations-2/.

Blumenfeld, S., Anderson, G., & Hooper, V. (2020). Covid-19 and employee surveillance. *New Zealand Journal of Employment Relations, 45*(2), 42–56.

Bodiat, A. (2020, April 17). No, I'm not 'just' a stay at home mom. Retrieved from https://www.nytimes.com/2020/04/17/parenting/stay-at-home-mom.html.

Budge, J., & Charles, M. (2020). Trends in support for stay-at-home mothering. *Contexts, 19*(2), 71–73.

Burkeman, O. (2018). Dirty secret: why is there still a housework gender gap? Retrieved from https://www.theguardian.com/inequality/2018/feb/17/dirty-secret-why-housework-gender-gap

Butler, S. (2020, April 6). Coronavirus lockdown to hit low-paid, young and women hardest, warns IFS. Retrieved from https://www.theguardian.com/business/2020/apr/06/coronavirus-lockdown-to-hit-low-paid-young-and-women-hardest-warns-ifs.

Charlton, E. (2020, June 4). COVID-19 lockdowns hit working mothers harder than working fathers. World Economic Forum. Retrieved from https://www.weforum.org/agenda/2020/06/covid19-lockdown-working-mothers-gender-gap/.

Cohn, D., & Caumont, A. (2017, April 8). 7 key findings about stay-at-home moms. Retrieved from https://www.pewresearch.org/fact-tank/2014/04/08/7-key-findings-about-stay-at-home-moms/.

Cook, J. (2018, January 31). Way more millennial women are becoming stay-at-home moms vs Gen Xers, but why? Retrieved from https://www.romper.com/p/

are-millennial-moms-staying-at-home-more-than-gen-x-moms-their-numbers-are-on-the-rise-8064295.

Crabb, A. (2019, September). Men at work: Australia's parenthood trap. *Quarterly Essay.* QE: 75.

Douglas, S., & Michaels, M. (2005). *The mommy myth: The idealization of motherhood and how it has undermined all women.* New York: Simon and Schuster.

Gale, R. (2017, October 11). How milleinails do stay-at-home motherhood. Retrieved from https://www.refinery29.com/en-us/2017/10/175528/stay-at-home-moms-modern.

Hays, S. (1996). *The cultural contradictions of motherhood.* New Haven: Yale University Press.

Hinsliff, G. (2020, June 23). The coronavirus backlash: How the pandemic is destroying women's rights. Retrieved from https://www.theguardian.com/lifeandstyle/2020/jun/23/the-coronavirus-backlash-how-the-pandemic-is-destroying-womens-rights.

Home Instead (2019). Crisis in caregiving: Workers who care for ageing parents face personal and professional obstacles. Report prepared for Home Instead: Senior care. Retrieved from https://www.caregiverstress.com/wp-content/uploads/2019/07/Working-Caregivers-Executive-Summary-0719-V4.pdf.

Lundram, S. (2018). More millennial women are becoming stay-at-home-mums – Here's why. Retrieved from https://www.forbes.com/sites/sarahlandrum/2018/02/09/more-millennial-women-are-becoming-stay-at-home-moms-heres-why/?sh=5b-2d42ef6a2b.

Manor, S. (2021). Being a working grandmother, mother, and daughter at the same time: A "Double Sandwich" in a four-generation family. *Journal of Family Issues, 42*(2), 324–344.

O'Brien Hallstein, D. L. (2017). Introduction to mothering rhetorics. *Women's Studies in Communication, 40*(1), 1–10.

O'Reilly, A. (2019). Maternal theory: Patriarchal motherhood and empowered mothering. In *The Routledge companion to motherhood* (pp. 19–35). London: Routledge.

Porter, E. (2019). Why aren't more women working? They're caring for parents. Retrieved from https://www.nytimes.com/2019/08/29/business/economy/labor-family-care.html

Power, K. (2020). The COVID-19 pandemic has increased the care burden of women and families. *Sustainability: Science, Practice and Policy, 16*(1), 67–73.

Schulte, B. & Swenson, H. (2020, June 17). An unexpected upside to lockdown: Men have discovered housework. *The Guardian.* Retrieved https://www.theguardian.com/us-news/2020/jun/17/gender-roles-parenting-housework-coronavirus-pandemic.

Singleton, J. (2000). Women caring for elderly family members: Shaping nontraditional work and family initiatives. *Journal of Comparative Family Studies, 31*(3), 367–375. Retrieved June 30, 2021 from http://www.jstor.org/stable/41603703.

Summers, H. (2020, June 19). UK society regressing back to 1950s for many women, warn experts. Retrieved from https://www.theguardian.com/inequality/2020/jun/18/uk-society-regressing-back-to-1950s-for-many-women-warn-experts-worsening-inequality-lockdown-childcare.

Todd, S. (2020, October 5). 1 in 4 women are considering stepping back from their career because of COVID-19. World Economic Forum: Agenda. Retrieved from https://www.weforum.org/agenda/2020/10/women-career-gender-equality-pandemic-childcare-parity-work.

Tong, K. (2019, November 8). Australia's 'man drought' is real – especially if you're a Christian woman looking for love. Retrieved from https://www.abc.net.au/news/2019-11-08/australia-talks-man-drought-real-especially-for-christian-women/11682002.

Waring, M. (1989). *If women counted: A new feminist economics.* London: Macmillan.

Women's Agenda (2019, November 28). More carers' leave may help Australians look after elderly parents and stay in work. Retrieved from https://womensagenda.com.au/latest/more-carers-leave-may-help-australians-look-after-elderly-parents-and-stay-in-work/.

# 8 "You should have asked" – Do we still have a long way to go?

As women must be more empowered at work, men must be more empowered at home.

—Sheryl Sandberg, Lean In

### Lucy's dream

When she was about ten years old, Lucy used to play 'house' with her cousins and siblings. She pictured that one day she would have children, and perhaps a husband of her own. She also used to play 'shops' and 'school days' and act out the role of the shop manager, or teacher. Lucy always pictured having a career. She'd never really play the two games together. She never 'juggled it all' while being the shop manager. She never had a job, while being the 'mum' at the same time.

When Lucy was about 16 years old, she was achieving excellent grades at school. She wanted to go to University and ultimately get a career. She had a boyfriend, Tom, whom she would eventually marry. They used to talk about their dreams, and Tom often said he wanted to be a father. Tom was less ambitious than she was, and often said he would be a stay-at-home dad. Lucy was pleased to have someone who understood her, and would be there, by her side.

Once Lucy started working, she realised it wasn't going to be as easy as she and Tom had imagined. Sure, she was working hard, and ticking all the boxes at work, but she was watching her friends having children and realised they were a lot of work. So many of the fathers were not stepping up as much as she would want. At least she was comforted by Tom's desire to have children, and how supportive he was of her career. She knew he'd pull his weight once they had kids, and maybe even become a stay-at-home dad down the track.

When she was nearly 30, Lucy and Tom started trying for a baby, and after two years, eventually conceived. After such a long time, Lucy was delighted to find out she was pregnant. Due to complications in the pregnancy, she ended up having the baby, Charlie, early, and had to suddenly finish

DOI: 10.4324/9781003020554-9

working. She didn't get to sit around watching movies waiting to go into labour like all her friends did. Her baby was, thankfully, healthy, and she got to take him home with her.

Charlie was small and didn't feed well. Tom had two weeks off work, and then returned to his job. Lucy was so preoccupied with the baby's routine. Tom wasn't sure how he could help her, especially as she was breastfeeding, so he threw himself into his career, confident that Lucy would ask for support when she needed it. He had never done particularly well at school or even at University, so the positive feedback he was receiving at work at work motivated him to work even harder. He also knew it would benefit Lucy and Charlie, so he felt really good about it.

Lucy had initially intended on going back to work after six months, but she was not ready to put Charlie in day care because of his small size. Eventually she took 12 months off work. By this stage, Tom had been promoted, with a good pay rise. When Lucy was about to return to work, she suggested to Tom that she work part time for the first year back. He readily agreed – after all, he had gotten that promotion, so they could cover the costs, and he didn't want Lucy working full time if she thought it would be a struggle. He really cared for her and wanted her to be happy.

Charlie went into day care two days a week, and Lucy enjoyed having a new identity outside of the house. It was unfortunate, but she was not able to return to the same job she'd had before she'd had Charlie – it was impossible to do that role part time – but she was grateful to have a job that was interesting enough. It wasn't exactly where she wanted to end up, but it would do… for now.

Tom kept working hard, often bringing work home at night. Because Lucy was working part time, she still did most of the household tasks on her days off, juggling it around Charlie's routine. Tom didn't expect Lucy to do it all, she just felt bad that he was working so hard, and she was only working two days a week. He would cook dinner on the weekends, and sometimes take Charlie out so that Lucy could have a sleep in on a Sunday morning.

Soon, Tom's hard work paid off, and he was rewarded with an even bigger promotion, leading a large Department. Lucy was thrilled for Tom, but as he travelled more frequently, attended more late-night meetings, and brought more work home, she wondered whether it was crazy for her to even consider working full time, especially since they wanted another child. They bought a larger house. After Lucy had their second child, she suggested to Tom that he should become a stay-at-home dad, so that she could work on her career goals. He gently said he would love nothing more than to stay at home with their children, but now his income was so much higher than hers, and they had the new house to pay for. He couldn't really stop working, but he said they could afford for her to not work if she didn't want. Also, he said, they could even afford a cleaner, so she could just enjoy her time off.

Whenever Lucy was frustrated about doing it all, Tom said "just let me know how I can help" or would say "but, we have a cleaner". It was very simple to Tom.

## Can we have it all?

Lucy's story is so much more common than we imagine. We see women working part time, and they say they've chosen to do this. They enjoy the flexibility. While this might be the case, it can sometimes be a forced choice. It can sometimes be the only real option.

Of course, Lucy could have worked full time. Many women do, even those with career husbands. It would be much harder, though, juggling the travel demands, evening functions, and work at home with young children. Lucy made a choice to work part time, not because she didn't want a career, but because she knew her life would be incredibly stressful if she threw herself into her work like Tom had while she'd been on maternity leave.

In writing this book, we have talked with hundreds of women, and observed even more, as they make career choices, and relationship choices. We have seen this pattern, and others, play out many times. Tom wasn't doing anything wrong. He didn't believe that just because he was male and she was female, Lucy should be doing the work at home. Actually, Tom thought he was using his time wisely while his wife was busy. He adores Lucy and is happy to pitch in, whenever she asks for help. The trouble was, he couldn't see what needed doing. In other words, Lucy carried the burden of the 'mental load' of running the household, as well as the burden of most of the household tasks, the childcare, and all decision-making around the children. The list, no doubt, goes on. On top of all of that, she was working part time in a job she enjoyed, but also trying to work out how to grow her career even more – at least to return to where she was before she had Charlie.

Lucy was the default carer in this case because Charlie had greater needs in his first year than they'd expected. Then it had become the logical choice, financially.

One of the challenges of being a woman in the modern world is that no matter how far we've come in equality, women still, generally, bear the burden of the 'mental load' of running a household, and/or managing a family. It can happen bit by bit. A small career break, a few years part-time, while our partner's career is progressing and suddenly it's the most logical choice for the woman's career to be secondary to the man's. This is not always the way – we've talked to plenty of females who are the main or sole breadwinner, too– but it seems to be a very common story when talking about juggling two careers. Even in relationships where the couple do not have children, there is the burden of the mental load that someone has to carry. It might be a little more equitable, although our research shows us that even in heterosexual relationships without children, women tend to bear the brunt of the mental load. This is how women have become known for multitasking! Also, when women carve out time for 'deep work' – a time for focused work on a particular project – we can be masters at cramming it in and getting whatever is needed to be done in the time required! The three authors of this book regularly draw on principles of deep work to get their tasks done – indeed, writing this book has occurred during many of our 'deep work' moments.

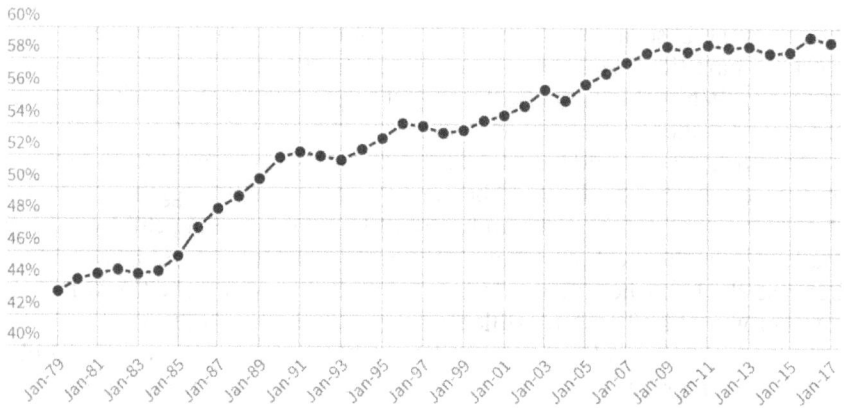

Source: ABS 2017

*Figure 8.1* Female labour force participation rate.
Source: Australian Bureau of Statistics (2017); Ting (2017).

The data tells us that women today are doing more than our mothers did (Ting, 2017). We all know that more women are in the workforce than ever before. More women are working full time than ever before. Less than a quarter of women worked in the early 1970s, compared to two thirds today (British Broadcasting Corporation – BBC, 2011). Figure 8.1 shows us Australian female labour force participation rates from 1979 to 2017.

Women are also better educated and are 'catching up' to men in terms of post-school education (Figure 8.2).

The good news is that this results in many women in better careers. Despite all of this, the kids still need to get to school (when a woman has children, that is!), dinner still needs to be on the table, lunches need to be made, groceries need to be purchased, and as we have already shown you, women still tend to carry the brunt of that, even though men are, increasingly, stepping up. This means our lives are busier than ever before.

You may have also heard that women today are spending more time with their children than women in the 1970s – this potentially surprising finding was reported by women in a survey in 2011 (BBC, 2011). They indicated that they spent more hours with their children than their mothers had. While this may be the case, we need to consider why it may be the case. Children in the 1970s were more likely to roam the streets, playing with friends in the neighbourhood, and organising impromptu sporting matches. When they had extracurricular activities, they took the bus, or went on foot, and parents were not necessarily expected to attend. These days, parents generally organise 'play dates' for their children, through back-and-forth phone calls, text messages, and calendar checking, something that was never really the

9: Non-school qualifications, by sex, 2004-2020(a)

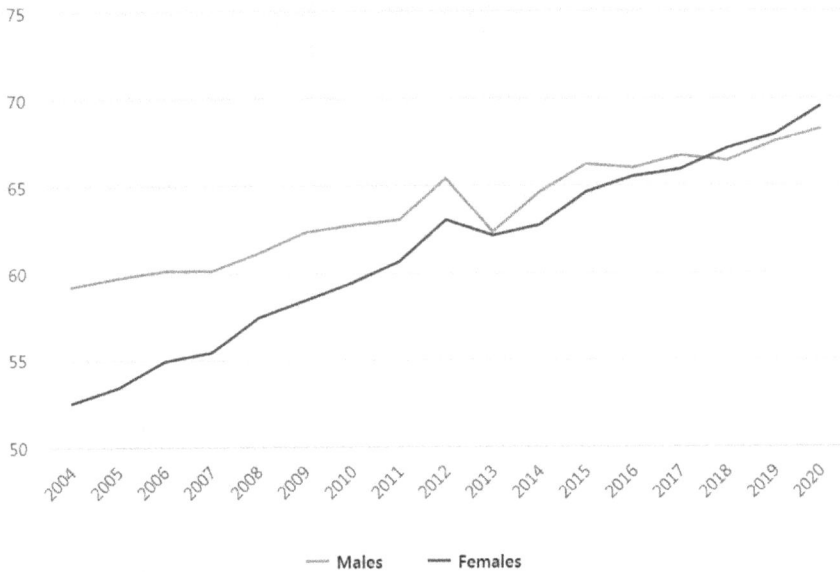

— Males  — Females

(a) All persons aged 20-64 years.
Source: Education and Work, Australia, 2020, Table 24

*Figure 8.2* Share of men and women with a non-school qualification.
Source: Australian Bureau of Statistics, ABS (2020).

case 30 or 40 years ago. Parents today drive their children to sport and other extracurricular activities. They are present when the child is signed up, and often attend matches and classes. Yet, when we really examine the data, we can see that mothers today have much more 'sedentary' time compared with mothers in 1965. Mothers today are more likely to spend time in front of a computer, the television, driving, or 'supervising' children at their sports matches or play dates. In contrast, in 1965, mothers were more 'active' – cooking, cleaning, playing with children, and exercising. While women still cook, clean, play and exercise, the increased use of technology (e.g., Dish-washers, cooking appliances) has reduced a lot of the 'activity' component of these tasks (Khazan, 2013).

Nevertheless, data indicates women today spend more time with their children than mothers in the 1970s did, and regardless of how the data is interpreted, women are busy. Woman are generally trying to do many things at once, and it is essential that for partnered people, tasks need to be shared to support the increasing roles of women in the workforce. As the quote at the start of this chapter states, "As women must be more empowered at

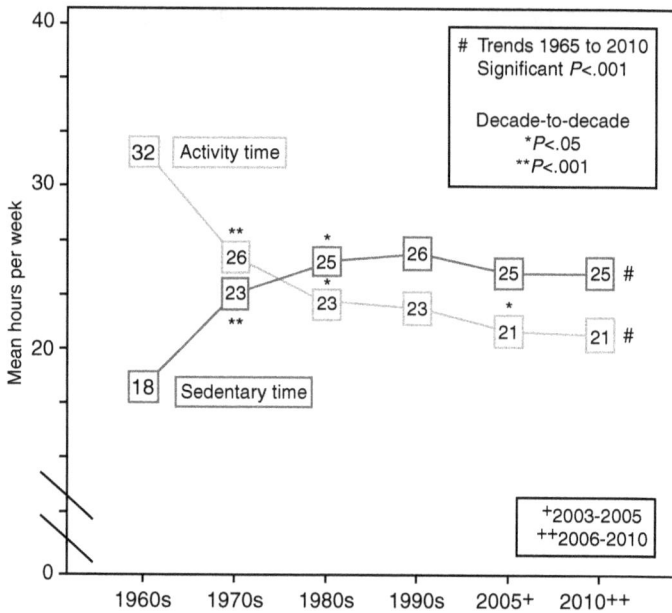

*Figure 8.3* Activity and sedentary time among moms with older children.
Source: Archer et al. (2013) from the Mayo Clinic Proceedings.

work, men must be more empowered at home" (Sandberg, 2013). This needs to be happening now – women should not be carrying the lion's share of home duties if a couple has dual careers.

When we talk about partnered people, the 'mental load' seems to be carried by one person over another in any household, and according to our research, this seems to be the case even in many same sex relationships. Of course, there's more equity in some relationships than others. What makes those relationships more equitable? Why do some partners not step up? Could it be the illusion of having things under 'control' that prevents the other partner from stepping up, or are they basing their behaviour at home based on what they saw in their family of origin and opting not to step up, because in their family of origin, one person had it under control? Although we did not interview males in the writing of this book, a number of the women we spoke with felt that the illusion of control could be the issue in a more equitable allocation of household tasks and sharing the mental load. The men thought these women had it 'all under control', often because the women indicated they liked things done a certain way. Other women didn't care about 'how' things were done as long as they were. This raises several questions.

What makes people more willing to 'hand over the baton' of control, regardless of the outcome – even if a task isn't done exactly how they would have done it themselves? Is that all based on personality trait?

Is one option for getting more men to take on the mental load about flexible work options for both partners? The boxed example (Box 8.1) shows a heterosexual couple sharing the load in many regards, as they both work part time:

---

## BOX 8.1  BELINDA IN HER FIGHT FOR FLEXIBLE WORK

Belinda is a 41-year-old woman with four children. Her husband and her have balanced part time roles between them to have as much time as possible with the children and to 'share the load' as much as they can. After years of trying to negotiate flexible work, she finally 'won' her case to work flexibly. She will work a nine-day fortnight between home and the office. The day she was offered the schedule, she said "I am so excited – I almost cried. It has really just been such a long process to get here".

We spoke to her before the decision had been reached. She explained how they balanced dual careers, work, a large family, and what they were hoping for in terms of flexible work:

"I had my first child seven years ago, I was an older parent – geriatric pregnancy was the term used by the medical profession and yes, that made me feel very old – and well into establishing myself in my career. Shortly after my first child was born (eight weeks to be precise), I was asked if I was interested in running a project that was exactly what I had been working towards and a great opportunity for me and so I accepted not knowing just how much an impact this would have on my life.

"I was very much torn between wanting to continue working on the career I had worked so hard for and being a full-time parent for my child. When I returned to work full time, my husband took over my parental leave and became a stay-at-home dad for a time.

"A year and a half later and my second child was born, and the position I was working towards became available. I applied, won the position and started when number two was four months old. Again, full time in a role that was very involved and required a lot of hours.

"After child number three was born, I decided that I didn't want to rush back to work and I took the time to have some maternity leave and enjoy being a parent and also had child number four during this time. My role is probably what you would describe as middle management, I'm responsible for a small team but have a higher level manager above me.

"When number four was about six months old, there were some changes at work and feeling ready to return, I decided to go back – full time to start with and then a plan to drop to part time about six months after my return. It was there that my struggles really took hold, although working for a company where the Enterprise Bargaining Agreement (EBA) states there are a variety of flexible working options, I had to fight to be granted any flexible working conditions. "This involved escalating requests to executive management for something that would be considered a reasonable request.

"Due to resistance from management to allow flexible working conditions, this then resulted in some pretty horrible working conditions and I ended up on stress leave. It was a very hard experience, I had people messaging me about how I should put my big girl boots on, be thankful I had a job and just suck it up to people telling me that I should stay home full time, get something closer to home, take a lower-level job because I have kids now, and that they should be my priority. These comments were mostly from women – some with young children, some with grown children, and some without. People who you feel should at least have some understanding of what you are going through.

"It was a very lonely and isolating experience and something I never even knew about let alone considered when I first became a parent. I took for granted the organisations I chose to work for had flexible conditions in their EBA and that it wouldn't be such a battle to access these.

"I would go through extremes feeling like maybe they were right and I should just leave and get something lower level to concentrate on being a mum to being angry that I should be made to feel like I had no right to the conditions in my award and that I needed to make a stand for every woman out there so they didn't have to go through the same situation as me.

"I really am very lucky that I have a very supportive husband who fully supported me when I was going through this process. I have no idea how parents without a strong support network manage these situations. My children are still young but as they grow, I know that I made the right decision in standing my ground.

"My husband and I have been able to both work part time so we can both spend time with our children while they are young but we are now in a position where we want to return full time. Again, my husband's employer is very supportive of this and I have been met with some resistance but I feel there is a change in this current review (fingers crossed)".

Belinda's example is particularly inspiring because it shows more equality than many heterosexual couples seem to demonstrate. They work together, and equally, to raise their four children and both have careers. We reached out to Belinda because Raechel is friends with her and has always been impressed by the apparently equal way they 'juggle it all'.

## Juggling it all

The topic of 'the mental load' is one that has increasingly emerged in the traditional media and on social media. Coining it 'the mental load' meant we suddenly had the language to describe something that women have understood for hundreds of years. While many women report that their husbands are 'good' around the home, or 'step up', there still seems to be a tendency for one person to manage the knowledge of what needs to be done, and when, and that one person tends to be a woman in a heterosexual union. Where there is a male and female couple without children earning the same money, a female is still likely to do four more hours of housework per week than her male partner. For equal-earning heterosexual couples with children, women are likely to do seven more hours of housework per week compared to their male partner and an additional seven hours of childcare per week (ABC Life, 2019). A female main breadwinner with children is still going to do more work around the home than their male partner – on average, five more hours of housework, and eight hours more childcare than their male partner (ABC Life, 2019), despite her earning more. In addition, even when men step up, they're frequently 'reminded' by the woman to pay particular bills, vaccinate the dog, get the dinner out of the freezer, or turn the oven on-that's the mental load that we are seeing increasingly being discussed by women, on social media and in the traditional media. Research shows that carrying the mental load results in lower relationship satisfaction and impacts on mothers' well-being. Almost 90% of women in committed relationships report feeling solely responsible for organising the family's schedule, and over 70% of working mothers feel responsible to stay on top of the schedules of their children. Over 50% of mothers report feeling exhaustion and burnout as a consequence of this pressure (Gonsalves, 2020). According to Crabb (2019), while nearly 50% of Australians in a recent Australian Talks Survey reported they were feminists, one in five believe society would be better off if more women stayed home with their children. We ponder why it wasn't reported if society would be better off if women OR men stayed home with their children!

We believe that maybe the mental load is increasingly being discussed because men are actually doing more. Yes, you read that right. We believe that as men are stepping up more, and women are physically doing less, while juggling their work, they are suddenly realising they still hold the responsibility for the reminders, for making sure it all happens, that there is food in the fridge, detergent in the laundry, and clean uniforms for the children.

And that is why we have begun to discuss it. That is why the inequity has emerged.

Some couples seem to have worked out a way to 'share the load'. Belinda, the 41 year old with four children discussed in the boxed example earlier in this chapter, expressed how important it was to share the load and have time for herself to build her happiness. She states:

> At home, we share the load really, my husband does the majority of the cooking, we both share homework duties, cleaning etc. While the kids were younger, we did utilise a cleaner for a period of time to take some of the load off. Free time for me, I used to do a lot of photography pre kids but found when they were younger I didn't really get a chance for that, so I have tried a number of different creative outlets. I discovered some group painting afternoons that I found really helped me take time out for me and shut off from everything that was going on. It was really nice to be able to get out of the house and focus on something that I enjoyed doing and then to have a piece of finished art at the end that resembled what it was meant to be really rewarding. I don't always make enough time for myself, but I definitely feel a difference in myself when I have made sure I have done something for me.

We asked Belinda why her husband steps up more than the average man – even down to the mental load – and rather than answer on his behalf, she got him to get in touch with us, which was yet another illustration of how it all works. He explained:

> because I'm a decent bloke and I love my family and I want to be there for them. But also I came from a broken home and I had to move out when I was fifteen. And I saw other kids who had a complete family – both their mum and dad were there for them, and even as they grew, their parents were there for them. They regularly went over for dinner, a visit, Christmas and so on and that's what I want for my family.

## The same-sex couple advantage?

If women tend to carry the mental load, and allocation of tasks is often arbitrarily based on gender norms, what happens in same-sex relationships? See boxed example (Box 8.2 Ella's story)

Ella's example shows us that before we start thinking about equitable division of labour – and the mental load – we need to consider how we do things.

We are certainly not suggesting one way is better than the other. Rather, it is important to recognise that 'your' way is simply 'one way'. If it's the 'only way' it does make it harder for your partner to take over the mental load. It's probably one of the biggest issues we see when we talk with women – they

---

**BOX 8.2 ELLA'S STORY**

Ella said "Part of the reasons I was keen to talk about my story is that I'm in a same-sex relationship, and I've noticed many of my friends struggling with gender-based expectations in their relationships and household management. I was feeling a little smug, thinking same sex couples had it all worked out, and I was keen to talk to you about it. My partner is a stay-at-home mum, and I'm a busy working mum, and I thought we had it all worked out.

"Then, the other day, I 'stepped up'. I mean, I always step up, but I step up to get them to follow the routine. "Have your breakfast". "Shower time now", and so on. I bath, dress and feed the toddler, I cook the dinner. She does, too. So, I tend to feel fairly confident – I'm always stepping up.

"On this particular day, though, I told my children to do something – I can't even remember what it was, maybe put their school uniforms in the wash or something. Their other mother, the primary carer, came out and questioned them, asked them why they were doing whatever they were doing. "Well, mama Ella told us to", they said. She gave me a look that said, without words, "why would you tell them to do that?" I smiled and said "you're always telling me to just step up. I stepped up". The trouble is, I hadn't stepped up the way she had imagined. She has a system. I took the mental load off her, but it wasn't 'right'.

"My partner is very organised and has a 'way' of doing almost everything. 'Her way'. For some people having their 'way' makes total sense. For me, done = good, and I don't care 'how' it is done.

"Next time I'll just ask her what she wants done".

---

want things done their way, but then get upset that they have to tell their partner what needs doing and how.

To have true equality, and equal stepping up in a relationship, there has to be no 'right' way or wrong way. There has to be seamless options for people to step up. From the hundreds of interviews we did with women, we would conclude that the couples that had the most equal allocation of tasks and mental load were ones that didn't seem to have a system, were happy to let things go, and were generally relaxed about things getting done provided they got done. Then everyone felt free to pitch in, children included.

This chapter has shown how women are increasingly busy – between work, study, raising children (if they have them) and home-related tasks, among other things. Burn out was another issue raised in a number of the interviews, and that led us to consider tips to reduce burn out. For each person, self-care will look differently. Belinda suggests holidays may help. She says:

I am still doing the juggle but my husband and I have devised a very clear plan on what we are working towards and this helps keep us focussed. We have promised ourselves that we will make sure we take regular holidays so we don't get burnt out and so we can spend quality time with the kids. For the first time in a long time, I feel like I have been able to take charge of my life's direction and it is such a different feeling to what had become the norm over the last seven years.

—Belinda

Other strategies to reduce burnout can include having a regular routine for sleeping, eating well, and exercising regularly. Knowing yourself, including triggers for burnout and activities that fulfil you will result in better 'self-care' (Saunders, 2019). For example, some people will enjoy a dinner out with a couple of close friends when they are feeling burnt out, while for others, the mere idea of this would be exhausting, and they'd much prefer a long soak in a bath, or an hour long walk around the neighbourhood. For some people, having a list of activities to rejuvenate themselves can be helpful, so that when they are feeling anxious, down, or stressed, they can glance at the list and pick something to perk themselves up a bit. Some people find putting them in categories based on how long each one takes could be helpful. There is a big difference between grabbing a five-minute phone call to a close friend through to doing a 1,000 pieces jigsaw puzzle, or creating a new artwork, but all of these can relax someone and make them feel a little happier.

## Ways to address the mental load emphasis on women

As we commenced writing this book, we felt it was one thing to merely identify the issues around the mental load, and another thing entirely to 'solve' it. We certainly don't have all the answers, so cannot solve the age-old issue, but there are a number of strategies for reducing inequities within the house.

One of the strategies women should follow is to offer their partner concrete examples of the mental load – not just "I do everything" or "I have to think of everything" but actual examples. Also, be sure that the planning work is discussed whenever you have a household chore discussion. For some couples, this might be done weekly, as they look at the week ahead and what the steps are. Recognise things don't have to be done 'your' way, as long as they're done, and finally, have regular chats about what is going on for you each week. In the couples that seemed to have the most equitable allocation of the mental load, task allocation might have shifted from week to week, based on each person's schedules and what needed to be done.

There are plenty of tips out there in the media, and some should be addressed by couples, and others by organisations – these examples are just some strategies which may help (See Box 8.3) below.

---

**BOX 8.3 SOME STRATEGIES TO REDUCE MENTAL LOAD**

Strategies for addressing the mental load:

- Talk about the mental load with friends, partners, and people in your workplace
- Both of you should take parental leave if possible, so that you are sharing the load from the start
- Do handover meetings at the end of maternity leave, end of each day, and so on, so that each of you feels empowered to step up
- Be willing to let go and let your partner take charge on some tasks
- Don't assume your way is better. Your partner's way may be different, but it still gets done
- When you're both home with the children, share the load for who is responsible for them, so that you can concentrate on other tasks when you're 'off duty'
- Delegate specific tasks and activities including all planning
- Develop a shared plan in advance eg. When planning for a trip, so that you can both step up and work toward the plan
- Organisations should consider the mental load in forms, processes, product design and Government policy. Implement systems to minimise this as much as possible

Source – A number of these recommendations were from Carrell (2019) and The First Five Years (2019).

---

## Reference list

ABC Life (2019). What do you do when you're sick of carrying the mental load for your household? Retrieved from https://www.abc.net.au/life/when-youre-sick-of-carrying-the-mental-load-for-your-household/11292628.

Australian Bureau of Statistics (2020). Education and work, Australia. Retrieved from https://www.abs.gov.au/statistics/people/education/education-and-work-australia/latest-release.

Australian Bureau of Statistics (2017, January). 6202.0 – Labour Force, Australia, January 2017. Retrieved from https://www.abs.gov.au/AUSSTATS/abs@.nsf/DetailsPage/6202.0Jan%202017?OpenDocument.

Archer, E. et al. (2013). Maternal inactivity: 45-year trends in mothers' use of time. Retrieved from https://www.mayoclinicproceedings.org/article/S0025-6196(13)00828-8/fulltext.

British Broadcasting Corporation (BBC) (2011). 1970s and 1980s 'were the best time to raise children'. Retrieved from https://www.bbc.com/news/education-12667107.

Carrell, R. (2019). Let's share women's mental load. Retrieved from https://www.forbes.com/sites/rachelcarrell/2019/08/15/lets-share-womens-mental-load/?sh=496639376bd6.

Crabb, A. (2019). Australian women worry more than men about (almost) everything. Retrieved from https://www.abc.net.au/news/2019-10-18/annabel-crabb-australia-talks-women-worried-more-than-men/11562860

Gonsalves, K. (2020). What is the mental load? The invisible labor falling on women's shoulders. Retrieved from https://www.mindbodygreen.com/articles/what-is-the-mental-load.

Khazan, O. (2013). Modern moms aren't as busy as 1960s moms were. Retrieved from https://www.theatlantic.com/health/archive/2013/12/modern-moms-arent-as-busy-as-1960s-moms-were/281997/

Sandberg, S. (2013). *Lean in: Women, work, and the will to lead*. New York: Alfred A. Knopf.

Saunders, E. (2019). Avoid burnout before you're already burned out. *The New York Times*. Retrieved from https://www.nytimes.com/2019/11/06/smarter-living/avoid-burnout-work-tips.html, accessed 14 May 2021

Ting, I. (2017). Young women in the 1970s versus today – Who has it better? Retrieved from https://www.smh.com.au/national/young-women-in-the-1970s-versus-today--who-has-it-better-20170307-gus6bw.html.

The First Five Years (2019). Mental load: How to share the mental load. Retrieved from https://www.firstfiveyears.org.au/lifestyle/mental-load-how-to-share-the-mental-load

# 9    Female leadership

What I am absolutely confident of is it will be easier for the next woman and
the woman after that and the woman after that. And I'm proud of that.
—Julia Gillard, Australia's first female Prime Minister upon
the conclusion of her time as Prime Minister 2013

## The career journey of female leaders

Despite increased rates of working women and career progression for
women, women are still considerably less represented in leadership positions
compared with men. According to the Australian Government's Workplace
Gender Equality Agency (WGEA):

– Women hold 14.1% of chair positions and 26.8% of directorships and
  represent 17.1% of CEOs and 31.5% of key management personnel
  (WGEA, 2020).
– 34.0% of boards and governing bodies have no female directors (WGEA,
  2019). By contrast, only 0.9% had no male directors (Australian Institute of Company Directors Statistics, 2020, 2021).

This is not due to lack of qualifications. In fact, of Australian women aged
20–24, 91.1% have completed year 12 education or above, compared with
88.8% of males (ABS, 2019). Furthermore, 58.7% of domestic University
enrolments are by females (DET, 2020). There is considerable contem-
plation about why women are underrepresented in leadership positions,
in the media, in academic research, and in conversations around Board
Room tables – career breaks being identified as one of the major barriers
for many women. The book, 'Lean In' By Sheryl Sandberg suggests that
for women to 'lean in' to the conversation in organisations, men need
to provide more support in their homes, to truly allow women to have
more equality in the workplace. Before we wrote this book, we interviewed over 200 women, and we asked them about their roles in work and
family. What was surprising is that even in many dual career couples, or

DOI: 10.4324/9781003020554-10

women with executive positions, the default in heterosexual relationships was that the woman carried the bulk of the load at home. Even when a couple didn't have children, women still carried the heavier 'mental load', although tasks were often divided up more equitably than they have been in the past.

This is a very important point of note – Many men feel they are stepping up more than ever before. The evidence suggests that men are doing more household work more than they ever did in previous generations. But, the roles they do are task oriented. They are doing more work around the house, generally speaking – cooking dinner, bringing the washing in, grocery shopping and the list continues. But, in heterosexual relationships, women are still primarily carrying the burden of knowing what needs to be done, and when. We even spoke to women who said they had a 50/50 allocation of tasks in their household, but they still had to tell their male partner what needed to be done and when and taking full responsibility for the 'mental load'. This was generally different in same sex couples, with many same-sex couples reporting that they shared the load including the mental load in most cases.

In this chapter, we share stories of all different types of households – single with kids, dual career with kids, dual career with no kids, same sex parents, and others – and we particularly emphasise career-oriented women. Then, we move from the household to the workplace, and will discuss leadership roles of women, the glass ceiling, perceptions in the workplace, and trends emerging.

## At home: the mental load with a leadership career

Beth is a woman in a same-sex relationship with dual leadership careers (Beth is a senior manager, and her partner is a School Principal) and two children, in their teens. Beth grew up believing she would be married, with children, and in a career, however her unstable upbringing means her life outcome has been greater than she had ever anticipated. In her relationship, she and her partner share the mental load and household tasks equally, but it may vary at particular points in time. If one of them has a lot on at work, the other may step up a little more, and vice versa. Beth works hard in her career and at home, but feels she's always striving. She said "I don't think women with kids who work ever get to the point where they think they have done a good job and completed tasks. There is always so much to do". Beth feels she's achieving at work, so much that she doesn't put pressure on herself or feel a sense of imposter syndrome. She explained, "My career has been in high pressure 'pressure-cooker' environments, that is where I thrive. I don't put much pressure on myself because I know I'm working at capacity and am highly skilled". She does feel imposter syndrome in parenting, however, and puts some of this down to her childhood. Her ultimate goal would be to be in the office two or three days a week, and work remotely the rest of the time, so that she could be more present at home, and have a better balance in her life.

In comparison, Jenny, is in a heterosexual marriage, also with dual careers. She's a CEO of her own business and her husband is a Chief Financial Officer, and she carries the mental load in their relationship. Jenny stated:

> I carry the vast majority of mental load. My husband steps up in terms of the physical load when I travel. I'm travelling about a third of the time. But the mental load still largely falls to me. Tasks like the dishwasher, laundry and so on tend to be split fairly evenly.

Jenny and her husband have a six years old child. Jenny grew up imagining she would get married at around 25 years of age, have three to four children, and expected she would probably be a stay-at-home mum. Instead, she married at about 40, and had trouble conceiving, so ended up having just the one child. She puts a lot of pressure on herself in the workplace, and work performance, but tends to be more relaxed around household chores, stating "near enough is good enough". Despite working hard on her business, she recommends having a clear end to the working day and choosing priorities carefully – she schedules meetings around her son's school hours and prioritises time with him as often as she can.

Jenny and Beth both have children, careers, partners with careers, and both women strive to work hard in their careers. Interestingly, Beth, in a same sex marriage, feels a greater sense of 'sharing the load' – even in regards to the 'mental load' – compared with Jenny. Jenny, in her heterosexual marriage, feels she does a lot more in carrying the 'mental load' at home, even though her husband would say he definitely steps up.

Another CEO we spoke with was Annie. Annie and her husband have three children (24, 21, and 14). They live across two states but spend three out of four weeks together. Annie does considerably more household work than her partner, who does "very little". Now that the kids have gotten a bit older, they step up a little more. Annie puts very little pressure on herself, she is pretty relaxed in all areas of her life. She doesn't buy into 'imposter syndrome' at all, and in fact, feels that she is in total control of all aspects of her life. She encourages down time, and said, "Simply spend your free time doing what you love surrounded by the people who love you... this will recharge the flattest of human batteries". She will work on weekends if necessary but says

> I work to a list and I have a routine that I follow. If I've completed my list then I feel accomplished and can sleep well. Sometimes I have to work weekends to catch up but I try to turn off on weekends to get my mind a break.

Sienna, another woman we spoke to, worked a nine-day fortnight, to her husband ten-day fortnight. She is in a leadership career, while he is not. She said:

> Hubby does the garden and organises tradespeople. I do all of the inside jobs: washing, cooking, cleaning, ensure the kids are organised, the family schedule and so on. He has a lot more down time to relax and a lot more time with friends than I do.

This example was particularly eye-opening – Although Sienna works almost as many hours as her husband, she's in a leadership role, and still has to manage the household, while he handles some outdoor tasks.

Could there be more than gender that influences who carries the mental load? Jenny and her partner, Melissa, both work in full time Government roles, at about equal level. They have one child. Jenny carries "about 70% of the mental load". She says this is because she is the "most organised. Melissa likes to organise holidays because she likes to do that". Is it possible, then, that people step into the mental load position not because of their jobs, or their gender, but because of perceived efficiency at these tasks? However, society has certainly assumed the view that women are more efficient at these types of tasks. One piece of advice given for shifting the mental load a little on to the other partner is to just not become an expert in a particular task, or to just hand an entire task to their partner to manage. Melissa organises the holidays in full detail, handling that entire task. Perhaps there are other tasks that Melissa could manage, to shift the 70/30 split to something more like 50/50.

Even for single people, allocation of tasks can be an issue. Samantha is 43, single, with no children, but lives with a housemate. She said she'd never intended on having children, but thought she might be married at some point, even though she wasn't particularly keen on the idea. Samantha says "I tend to do more of the household tasks because my roommate is prone to depression and has issues with processing and functioning. This has meant that I tend to take over the mental load". She feels she has a good work life balance by not checking emails when she's not working and participating in her hobbies during her time off. She said to us,

> It is important to be selfish. Sometimes being selfish means saying no to a project when you're already overworked, or not attending an event that you don't really need to attend or blocking off an hour or two for your own personal needs. If you don't respect your own time, no one else will, so it's important to be selfish about how you spend it.

She says that a to do list really helps her manage it all.

> To-do lists are vital, with a sheet of paper divided into quadrants for Things to Do (tasks), Things to Write (usually freelancing projects,

but would depend on the person), Things to Buy (groceries, household goods), and Things to Remember (birthdays, appointments). Having phone calendar reminders are also necessary for me.

Olivia also doesn't have children, and never wanted them, but she has a male partner. Both are in leadership careers, in different roles. She states that they share the mental load fairly equally depending on what they have on at a particular time. Similarly, based on what they have on, or personal preferences, "Sometimes tasks are just shared – for example, he'll cook, so I'll wash up". Olivia feels their lives are well balanced because they generally work similar hours, have no children, and no real expectations based on gender.

These stories show you there is no 'one way' to manage things. Most importantly, in a relationship, or even a household with flatmates, task allocation should be openly discussed, and agreed upon.

This chapter highlights women in senior roles, and a lot of our discussion has focused on life at home for women. What about within the workplace? The next section of this chapter explores women in leadership roles.

## At work: women in leadership – emerging trends

Women are known to be 'transformational leaders' (Van Edwards, 2017), and female leaders tend to provide more mentoring and coaching than their male counterparts (Chamorro-Premuzic & Gallop, 2020; Gipson, Pfaff, Mendelsoh, Catenacci, & Burke, 2017). A transformation leader is one where they bring their team along with them, coach them, generally model behaviour, and emphasise teamwork and authentic communication (Van Edwards, 2017). Leaders can be more transformational by spending more time engaging with each staff member on an individual level and look to inspire greater motivation to reach the collective goal. Males, in contrast, tend to be more transactional, providing clear instructions so that team members meet expectations (Van Edwards, 2017). Research has shown that through transformational leadership, comfortable work environments and exceptional results emerge, through open communication and high levels of personal growth and motivation. Transactional leadership, on the other hand, allows teams more autonomy. Having a balance of these approaches can be beneficial (Van Edwards, 2017) and some evidence suggests a transformational style can be beneficial in female dominated industries while a transactional style may be more appropriate in a male dominated profession (American Psychological Association, 2006).

Interestingly, a US Gallop Poll study shows that the majority of Americans now have no gender preference for their boss (Figure 9.1).

The graph in Figure 9.1 shows that while there was a preference for a male boss in the 1950s to the 1990s, there was a decline in preference for male bosses from the late 1970s. From the early 2000s, there has been no gender preference for boss. If people don't tend to have a preference for gender of

**Majority of Americans Have No Gender Preferences for Boss**

If you were taking a new job and had your choice of a boss, would you prefer to work for a man or a woman?

PREFER MALE BOSS   PREFER FEMALE BOSS   NO DIFFERENCE (VOL)

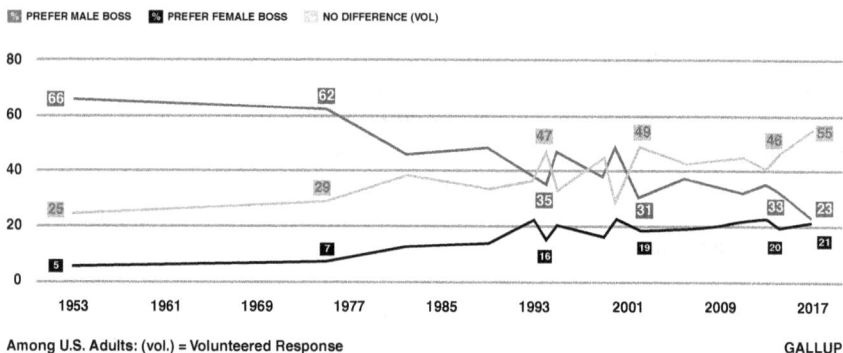

Among U.S. Adults: (vol.) = Volunteered Response

GALLUP

*Figure 9.1* Majority of Americans have no gender preference for boss.
Source: US Gallup Poll (2017).

leaders, it may indicate that there is less difference between male and female leadership than previously thought.

## Two leadership careers

Amber is 36 years old. She and her husband have a three-year-old child. Amber works four days a week, and lectures at university one night a week. Her husband works full time. Although Amber dreamt of a 'high-powered' leadership career as a child, her career has taken a back seat to her husband's. "I did not expect this to happen", she said, but then adds "I'm primary carer (to our child) which I did want". Despite this, both Amber and her husband have senior management roles – Amber's in finance and his in retail. We asked Amber who is charge of household tasks. She said that while she carries the mental load, her husband will participate in some tasks – he does all of his own washing, mows the lawn and purchases groceries. He also does cooking for the adults. Amber, on the other hand, does everything else, including all decision-making, research, cooking for their child, and all financial management. "It's tiring", she said, "and my biggest time management tip is that I don't sit down until all my jobs are done". It sounds exhausting, but Amber says she feels she "juggles it really well" – she doesn't ever work on her days off, and when she can, tries to exercise, or sit down to do some jigsaw puzzles or read a book. "I put a lot of pressure on myself. I like a spotless house. I've done a good job at home when I've done a number of activities with my child, the house is spotless and my jobs are done". Amber said she pressures herself less at work, mainly because "I've been there so long, and know what to do". She did say there's some pressure to do a good job, and states she measures success at work by positive feedback and providing value to her clients.

## Carla's story

"I didn't set out to become a leader, at least, it wasn't really a strategic plan. I have a strong work ethic, and my goal was just to work as hard and as effectively as I could. While leadership might have appealed, I simply found a career that I was passionate about in my mid-twenties, and I've moved up the ladder since. Over time, I would offer to lead something, or do something, and I'm always willing to pitch in. In a group, I'd glance around, and if no one was taking responsibility, "I would just jump in and coordinate things. I quickly recognised I had leadership traits, although I suppose it's something I've always had, I just got more confident about it over time.

"I commenced more formal leadership roles, and now I firmly see myself as a leader, but now I'm always telling people that you don't need a leadership role to be a leader. Anyone can be a leader and I encourage everyone to think about the impact they can have, their field of influence.

"I read a lot of books and literature about leadership. I think one of my biggest traits as a leader is authenticity, coupled with kindness and compassion. The literature talks about the difference between male and female leaders, and while I acknowledge there are different perceptions, and styles, I don't invest a lot of time in considering myself a 'female leader'. I'm just me.

"I'm just someone in a leadership role. I'm just someone who wants everyone to step up and be leaders, where they can. I'm just someone who loves supporting the people around me.

"In hindsight, I can't imagine not being a leader. Although I didn't necessarily set out to be in a leadership role, I can't really imagine not being a leader. Even without a formal title, I'd still be a leader".

## The Old Girls Club?

Carla mentions that although she never set out to be a leader, by doing the best job she could, and supporting those around her, a leadership career emerged. You'll often hear of the 'Old Boys Club' where males that know one another, or know of one another, will provide support and connections. Research has shown that this increases further connections. Women have typically never been good at it overall – research shows women are less likely to ask for help, particularly if they don't know the person they're needing to ask particularly well. Women also tend to separate friends and colleagues, while men just have 'networks'. Furthermore, men have a lot more men in senior positions to call upon, while women may have one or two senior contacts in their organisation or industry. As women move up the ladder, the ability for networking increases, but we believe in the importance of building strong networks of women, to enable greater connections, mentoring, and succession planning. Does your organisation have a women's mentoring program, or leadership program? One of the authors of this book was fortunate to be involved in a series of 'group mentoring' groups, where women worked together. It was incredibly powerful, and supportive. This may not be the ideal fit for you, though, or maybe it isn't possible in your industry or organisation. Is there a way you could mentor a junior female in your industry, or offer workshops? Consider options for this, and how it may help to increase opportunities for new female leaders.

## Managing the do list

As we talked to many women in leadership careers who seemed to be juggling many roles, we asked them for their best time management tips.

Sarah is 43 years old, married with two kids and is in a leadership role. Sarah said for time management, it was important to

> Plan! Create To do lists and review them regularly. Break a large job down into ten-minute chunks that you can fit in around your other work. Just as you break a project down month by month, week by week, set small easy goals. Just start it. Even if you stop and start many times. Keep learning a new skill or practice an old skill. Learn and share with others and they will encourage you to finish and complete your tasks toward your goal. I always rush through, or neglect housework so I have more time to read, study, volunteer, help and support others. If it's important you do that first. Everything fits in and around what you want to achieve.

Claudia is 41 years old. She's in a de facto relationship with a man, and they do not have children. Both her and her partner are academics, though she's a little more senior than he is. Claudia puts a lot of pressure on herself at work but tends to be relaxed at home. She told us that she used to be fanatical about having a tidy house, and has to clean it if it's too messy, otherwise she gets stressed, but it's no longer her top priority. As a teenager, Claudia didn't want to have children, however was open to changing her mind if she met a partner that wanted them. She always saw herself going to University, and having a career, and in fact, pictured becoming a University lecturer. She takes great pride in her work, never thinking she's done enough even when she knows she has. When we asked her about her to do lists, she said:

> the to do list is never complete and I always feel like I've dropped the ball on something. In my last job I knew I was doing lots of good things but as they weren't the 'right' things I often felt like a failure. My current job – I've been in it for 3 years – is less stressful but I often feel I'm not doing enough. I can look at my CV and see I work hard but I'm not sure how I measure success.

Claudia attends a lot of time management courses and will continue to do so. She always carries a to do list and plans her day around tasks. She sometimes uses a weekly planner so that she can see how best to balance her time across a week. In terms of household management, Claudia carries the mental load, but tasks are split between the two of them. She stated this as "he does a lot of cooking and some cleaning" and that she handles all household management (bills, knowing when they're running low on items, etc.) and "making sure we don't live in a bachelor pad". She is confident in her abilities and qualifications, stating, "I worked hard to get my PhD and I work hard in my job. I don't think its luck that I do what I do. I don't feel I have success – more. I've worked damn hard to get here and maybe now am getting some recognition for it. But I'm not sure I want all the recognition as I didn't do it alone and had lots of help along the way".

## Strategies for increasing participation of female leaders

In this chapter, we've explored rates of female leadership, biases for or against female leaders, and we've considered how leadership careers impact on juggling it all, including the mental load, which was discussed more in detail in Chapter 8.

To result in greater career equity, we need greater numbers of female leaders. To increase rates of female leaders, greater workplace flexibility is recommended. Mentoring from senior leaders, recruitment campaigns, and role models also help drive numbers of female leaders within an organisation. Organisations should be transparent about their diversity profiles, and gender equity, and create goals in relationship to leadership diversity. However, female leadership shouldn't just be addressed at an individual organisation level, but rather at a societal level. Government policies around childcare, parental leave (for all parents, not just a birthing parent) and flexible work support increase rates of participation by women in leadership careers.

We hope this book has provided you with some relevant reflections, and possible action steps, to make changes in your home, workplace, or just in your thinking. From the expectations on women, generally, through to expectations in the house, and the importance of supporting females in our industries. Start conversations about this. Reach out, support the women around you. It's one way we can make inroads to the inequities that have surrounded us for the years prior.

## Reference list

American Psychological Association (APA, 2006). When the boss is a woman. Retrieved from https://www.apa.org/research/action/boss.

Australian Bureau of Statistics (2019). Gender indicators, Australia, Nov 2019, 'Table 4.5: Attainment of a Bachelor Degree or above by age, 2007 to 2017', data cube: Excel spreadsheet, cat. No. 4125.0. Retrieved from https://www.abs.gov.au/AUSSTATS/abs@.nsf/DetailsPage/4125.0Nov%202019?OpenDocument.

Australian Government Department of Education and Training (2020). Retrieved from http://highereducationstatistics.education.gov.au/.

Australian Institute of Company Directors Statistics (2020). We've reached a milestone: Over 30% of directors on ASX 200 boards are female. Retrieved from http://aicd.companydirectors.com.au/advocacy/board-diversity/we-have-reached-a-milestone-for-female-directors.

Australian Institute of Company Directors Statistics (2021). Board diversity statistics. Retrieved from http://aicd.companydirectors.com.au/advocacy/board-diversity/statistics.

This dataset noted that students who did not want their gender recorded as male or female were counted as female (see Australian Government Department of Education and Training (2020), Notes on the data). Retrieved from http://higher-educationstatistics.education.gov.au/DataNotes.aspx.

Chamorro-Premuzic, T., & Gallop, C. (2020). 7 leadership lessons men can learn from w. Retrieved from https://hbr.org/2020/04/7-leadership-lessons-men-can-learn-from-women.

Gipson, A. N., Pfaff, D. L., Mendelsohn, D. B., Catenacci, L. T., & Burke, W. W. (2017). Women and leadership: Selection, development, leadership style, and performance. *The Journal of Applied Behavioral Science, 53*(1), 32–65. doi:10.1177/0021886316687247.

US Gallup Poll (2017). Americans no longer prefer male boss to female boss. Retrieved from https://news.gallup.com/poll/222425/americans-no-longer-prefer-male-boss-female-boss.aspx.

Van Edwards, V. (2017). Battle of the sexes: Male vs. female leadership. Retrieved from https://www.huffpost.com/entry/battle-of-the-sexes-male-vs-female-leadership_b_59647ddbe4b09be68c00551a.

Workplace Gender Equality Agency (WGEA, 2019). Australia's gender equality scorecard 2018–19. Retrieved from https://www.wgea.gov.au/sites/default/files/documents/2018-19-Gender-Equality-Scorecard.pdf.

Workplace Gender Equality Agency (WGEA, 2020). WGEA Data Explorer, Workforce composition. Retrieved from https://data.wgea.gov.au/industries/1#gender_comp_content.

# 10 The end. Or the beginning

I wish I had a wife...

For women of my generation, it was the 'juggling act'. Jobs, marriage, children, homes and aging parents were the balls we added, tossing them up in the air as our lives filled up and praying they wouldn't come crashing down on our heads.

—Willow Bay

## The end. Or the beginning

For a long time, this book was, for each of us, a goal. An individual and collective pipe dream, something to do one day. We had all wanted to add to the conversation about the experience of being a woman in the early twenty-first century, the experience of juggling it all. We wanted to add to the conversation about equality, to talk about women's experiences, our experiences, and those of our friends, of trying to be superwomen, and about women succeeding in their goals, whatever those goals were. We were interested in why many women still seemed to juggle more than many men and explore what we saw as a very binary way of viewing the world, and indeed, dividing household tasks. And yet, we never got around to writing it. We would do it, eventually, when the marking was done, the kids were asleep, the dishes were done, the house was tidy, the washing wasn't piling up on the couch.

We knew writing a book was something that, as Virginia Wolf, described, relied on us having the opportunity, the time, the space to write. However, we also realised that, if we didn't reach out and grab that opportunity, that time and that space, we'd never get there. We had to make the opportunity, the time, and the space.

And that's kind of the whole point of the book. But, as we noted in earlier chapters, for most women, their day is no less hard than it has ever been for women. For the majority of the world's women, the time, or the space, or the money, or the childcare are luxuries they can ill afford but massively impact their day-to-day lives and their ability to live their dreams. What makes this doubly cruel is the exhortations to do it all, to have it all. As discussed

DOI: 10.4324/9781003020554-11

in the first chapter, mentioning the stickers we were given in high school proclaiming, "girls can do anything", it's not that simple. We need to ask ourselves, what does it mean to do "anything"? Is everybody's "anything" equally valued? The mother we spoke with who quit her job to look after having her children didn't stop facing criticism any more than the career woman we spoke with who didn't quit her job after having her children. The opposite-sex couples who reported many time management issues and the same-sex couples with their own issues. The trans women who face the discrimination like the discrimination the Indigenous women, migrant women, women with disabilities all face.

We all have busy lives – busier than ever before. We're working more than ever, and the 'flexibility' of our careers often comes at a cost, working at home late into the night, and responding to emails at 7am (or at the hospital while having a serious bone fracture set, as one of our authors recently did). We're in more senior jobs than ever before, and yet, our responsibilities at home haven't become any less time-intensive. As we noted in the book, we are doing more hands-on childcare now than ever before, and although men are stepping up more than they did, the gap between women's work and men's work hasn't really budged.

Women may have more help but just seem to do more. Whether that's parenting or caring, we're required to do more, because the world has changed. And men are doing more, too. In a heterosexual relationship, men are reportedly doing more tasks... they're changing nappies, emptying dishwashers, even cooking meals and handling the kids' bedtime... but where does the mental load fall? The research and evidence shows that, despite it all, it still falls predominately on women. That is the main thing that needs to change for anything at all to change.

In this book, we've talked about many different things – from data around the contemporary lives of women, to how women are represented in the media, and how the changing nature of work will impact on women. We've talked about women in leadership, and the roles women typically undertake. We've explored well-being, diversity, and constantly rushing and the impact of that on our health. We talked about Indigenous women, migrant women, and LGBTIQA+ women and non-binary people. We've talked about the current environment for women, and we've addressed the mental load in quite a bit of detail. We've identified strategies, too – strategies around addressing stress, the mental load, attitudes towards female leaders, the changing workplace, the fight for flexible work, and how the COVID-19 pandemic has exacerbated the need to address all of this.

While the data is all through the book, we think it's important to address in more detail where to from here, to map a way forward. We can't solve all the world's problems with one book, but by identifying the problems, we are making strides towards solving them, advocating for them, and acknowledging them in policy decisions, business decision-making, and household conversations.

## Indigenous women

The data shared in this book shows that Indigenous/First Nations women are more suspectable to issues such as domestic violence, incarceration, and having lower income jobs. Policy decisions around closing the gap are currently being addressed, however, more can be done. Broadly, we suggest that some of the problems are that interventions are done to Indigenous women, not by and for Indigenous women (Johns, 2021). If more services were operated by women, and were properly funded, these services could offer longer term strategies and solutions to the problems that have changed, and we acknowledge their improvement, but not enough. These support services need to be funded at federal level with quadrennial funding and operated at arm's length from government to ensure women who know what their community needs can make decisions that are in the best interests of community. These services need to consider the impacts of systematic racism, inequality in health and education, the impact of the stolen generations, continued policies that see Indigenous communities, as well as Indigenous women, policed more severely than other populations, as well as the ongoing harm of a system that removes Indigenous children at a rate that is 9.7 times the rate of white and non-indigenous children (SNAICC, 2020). We argue that one key strategy that can support Indigenous women participating in higher education and employment and support their children is to provide free childcare for the children of Indigenous women (Johns, 2021).

It is clear, from the data we presented in the previous chapters, that the current policy settings are not sufficiently helping Indigenous women, their children, or their communities. Working closely with Indigenous communities, and, in particular, Indigenous women, will help that. Undertaking co-creation workshops to determine solutions, rather than simply identifying problems, is imperative (Johns, 2021). In addition, understanding the heterogeneous nature of the Indigenous mobs in Australia, and considering how different mobs will need different and more nuanced services and supports can only happen on the ground.

Schools can also help, by providing specialised Indigenous teacher aides, by including language, through in-servicing on the specific needs of Indigenous students, their culture, and community. By understanding the support needs of this community, they will have the skills to succeed in education. Again, this needs to be devolved to community, and the community, women in the community, need to lead here and be trusted to show the way.

## Migrant women

As with all women who've experienced trauma and stressful life events, the issues faced by migrant women are myriad. There are mental health implications, the issues that arise from English not being a first language or dialect, the impact on their physical health from potentially escaping unstable governments, or difficult home environments. There are a lot of issues faced in this community. For instance, Loh & Klug (2017) found in their interviews with 30 migrant women that upon arrival to their host country, many of these women encountered a number of acculturation challenges. Nevertheless, the authors also found that many of these women, given time, displayed resilience and developed competencies to become highly productive citizens.

Again, funding is a factor, as is trusting them to lead the charge and tell us, the rest of the community, what their needs are. Research says, if we help women help their communities, the whole economy benefits, and of course, beyond that there are major benefits at individual, family, and community levels. We all benefit when women are successful (De Maio, Silbert, Stathopoulos, Rioseco, Jenkinson & Edwards, 2017), which explains why it is so important to trust women led initiatives. We also know, from the data in the previous chapters, that women are wanting to help but again, as with Indigenous women, it's up to governments to co-create solutions, fund the services and get out of the way. The different experiences of different migrant groups require us to think differently about how we help these populations. It requires us to trust women, and their communities, to lead.

## Trans women

One of the groups that has experienced many hardships in the community is trans women. As our data in the previous chapters shows, trans women experience discrimination, have much lower earnings, are more transient and are more likely to commit suicide and self-harm. Again, the need is to trust these women to explain their needs, to help us to understand what they are and to introduce policy settings that facilitate those needs being met. We need to consider how discrimination is intertwined in all of life from bathrooms to single-sex schools and how these issues affect all women, and especially trans women. For non-binary people, particularly, there is a need to be more inclusive, on forms, in business language, and in society. Even the everyday greeting of 'welcome ladies and gentlemen' can be very 'othering' for non-binary people, and we need to rethink our business communication, and decision-making. In fact, this binary approach was one of our hesitations about writing a book about 'women', but we felt it was necessary. It is also necessary to include trans women, and non-binary people, within our consideration of issues to empower our communities.

## LGBTIQA+ women generally

It would be a mistake to think that LGBTIQA+ women's issues ended with the gay-marriage vote in Australia in 2017. People in the LGBTIQA+ community still faces discrimination in society, in everything from trying to access reproductive services to simply being discriminated against in places as diverse as the job market and even, sometimes, on the bus. While there is evidence that Lesbian women out-earn straight women (Bagri, 2017), they still face many challenges in the market for jobs and opportunities (Fric, 2019) and families parented by same-sex couples still report facing discrimination (Fric, 2019), though it is improving.

## Women in heterosexual relationships

Women are able to earn a living, to have their own money, a bank account separated from their husband's and to choose to have children, but not all women have this experience. Many women in heterosexual relationships are still carrying the bulk of the physical, and mental load. In the earlier chapters we described how the work of women is growing, not shrinking, especially in heterosexual couples with children. Heterosexual women are doing more hours at work, and more hours at home. They are generally the ones who do all the work getting pre-school children skilled up and ready for school, and, when the children are at school, women as mothers take on the mental load of organising birthday presents, schlepping them to their activities and remember their friends' names. These women have seen both great gains, but these gains haven't necessarily translated to better experiences. They're still stressed, still juggling and still tired.

## Single women

Some single women have children, some do not, and others have empty nests, once the kids have grown up. Some are single women by choice – even from conception of their babies. Others have chosen to leave relationships that haven't been right for them, and other women have been left, through death or relationship breakdown. Even today, our interviews showed that single women can face societal discrimination, though many report that the ability to make all the decisions is empowering. It's also exhausting. Whether they have children, or not, the mental load falls completely on them, and means that there are constantly decisions needing to be made.

## Women generally

While we cannot speak for individual woman, we have always experienced varying degrees of stress, collectively. Women today are under greater levels of stress than ever before. Of course, there are some for whom this statement is anathema. How can we argue this? Unlike in Austen's day, women are not only able to have a bank account, to leave their husband and live as an independent woman, they're more likely to have the financial independence to do so. This independence breeds choices, and far more opportunities than ever before in human history, so whether we actually experience more stress than generations before us could be a contentious issue, and it's certainly not a competition. Nobody denies women had it tough when they had to shave soap to put into a vat of boiling water to wash clothes by hand, or one of our author's grandmothers who grew up in a London slum. In that anecdote, she described how the family had to wash on the stairs, never taking off all their clothing. That sounds frightening, but it's no less tough, in different ways, today. We may have washers and dryers and air conditioners and cars, but we still face discrimination and judgements and recriminations regardless of our choices.

What we do know, however, from looking at the data, and talking to hundreds of women, is that the juggle to do it all is stressful. The opportunities women have has resulted in pressure to do it all, to be everything. To be the best at our jobs, but be ever-present at home – in other words, many women strive to climb the ladder, one handed, while holding the baby in the other arm. We don't question this. In fact, women seem to feel more questioned when they prefer to opt out of climbing the ladder. The premise of this book is that women will make all sorts of choices, but it still comes down to that – a choice. We can't necessarily do everything at once.

One of the authors of this book has five children, and a senior academic role. When, in casual conversation with people she's working with, she mentions she has five young children, people are amazed. They inevitably ask how she's managed it all.

"My partner is at home with the kids", she admits, even though she does a lot of juggling of everything herself, a lot of late nights just to get it all done, and a constant to do list.

"Oh, wow. Isn't he amazing?" they say, envying her for how her husband steps up. "You're lucky".

"My partner is female", she adds, smiling, as if it matters.

"Oh", is often the simple response with a casual shrug, or an understanding sound of acknowledgement. Her partner is no longer deemed amazing because she is a woman. Instead, that's expected of her, and 'luck' is no longer part of the equation.

In fact, sometimes the conversation will continue, "I wish I had a wife...".

Another author of this book arrived in Australia as an international student. Her plan was to graduate and return to Canada but as faith would have it, she met her husband at the university when she was doing her postgraduate work. They started off as friends but became husband and wife after 10 years of knowing each other. The decision to be a couple was not taken lightly as the author was stressed about how people would perceive them as an interracial couple. To share with the readers of this book, among the many things she worried about was over food. The author grew up eating rice while her husband grew up on potato and chips. Imagine the horror of having to cook both rice and potato! Lucky for her, her husband is not a foodie and he basically eats whatever she cooks for him. In many ways, this stress was self-initiated. She has over the years learned to not worry so much about what or how others perceive her and her husband. When asked whether her husband is a white Caucasian man, she has learned to simply answer "yes", without feeling the need to further justify her decision. The author believes strongly that women, irrespective of where we come from have the right to make our own live decisions without being judged by men or other women.

## Policy issues

Every woman having a wife could be a great solution, but it's not the only way to support women. One of the best ways to support women is to create policies which enable more equal participation in the workforce, and in senior careers.

Policies would need to work on extending parental leave opportunities. In Australia, parental leave opportunities are now provided, however they are means tested. While there is partner leave, it is paid at a minimal wage and only covers two weeks. It would be useful that the policies are expanded to provide greater partner support, as partner participation in supporting the birthing parent during those heady early days of a child's life generally results in greater participation over time. Furthermore, it would be useful if eligibility didn't link to means testing the primary parent only – some women report that where the primary parent earns a high income, they are ineligible, while other primary parents in a relationship with a high-income earner are eligible. This results in inequity between families, and is seen to penalise high earning females, but not high earning males, generally speaking.

But, it's also policies that support women at the other end of the age spectrum. Women increasingly find themselves taking on the mantle of supporting and caring for older relations when they become infirm. There are no paid leave opportunities in Australia for that responsibility on which the community is no less dependent. The community benefits if people step up and undertake care work at any stage of the age spectrum, and therefore it should be equally supported when families take on the care of infirm, frail or elderly members. As we noted in the chapter on caring, increasingly women are finding that they are called on to do this work, which has massive implications for their careers, their incomes and their ability to save for their retirements.

Another issue is the gender pay gap. Studies find that, as an industry feminises, it is paid less, suggesting an issue with what work, and whose work, is valued. As Marilyn Waring noted in the 1980s, the failure to count women's work in GDP, when disasters (both natural and human caused) do count, is a major failure to properly estimate both the value of women and the work they do. She argued for us to consider policies that address not only the gender pay gap but also the ways those policies assume the unpaid work of women and fail to account, acknowledge and value it in the same ways we account for, acknowledge and value more male-centric work. If we listened to excellent scholars like Waring, we'd find ways to ensure we equalise pay and we value women's work, both paid and unpaid, in more equitable ways.

There is no denying that the wage gap exists and is evident in three ways: first, in many cases women get less pay for the same job as many men. Yes, we know that wages are frequently set at government level and that there are laws against paying different wages for the same work. But, as we describe in detail in "Pay gaps and time outs", the differences between male and female superannuation balances are evidence of the differences in the pay between the sexes. In addition, government diktats around pay and conditions can be overridden or ignored. For example, many wages are negotiated in bargaining agreements between employees and employers. Similarly, bonuses are not set at a government level. In more insidious practices in most industries, employees are discouraged from talking to each other about their pay rates which keeps differentiated pay hidden. Second, as we talk about in that same section, and in other places in the book that detail women's experiences of work and family, women are more likely than men to take career breaks or work part time mainly to care for children or elderly relatives. These decisions impact on their retirement funds, their accumulated savings and even their ability to nab a role as CEO. Third, careers traditionally seen as female dominated tend to attract less pay compared with careers that are traditionally seen as male dominated. As Ziwica (2021) notes about an Australian case for increasing the pay of highly trained but poorly paid care-home staff, when an industry shifts from being male dominated to being female dominated, the pay tends to stagnate and drop off so that the influx of female workers tends to reduce the pay in that occupation. But it is not just the increasing feminisation of a workforce that affects pay, it's also the feminisation of a role. Think of the similarity in training times between a police officer and a child-care worker or an aged-care nursing assistant but the different pay rates for each role. Each of these issues must be considered and addressed.

Finally, we believe policies should explore superannuation impacts on women, given they are more likely to step out of the workforce, or work part time, when raising children, or care for older relatives. While there are policies around contributions to superannuation, women are still more likely to have lower retirement balances. This needs to be addressed, through consideration about the issues women are facing, and solutions needs to be identified for greater equity.

There are numerous other areas where policies can support women. We encourage people to stand up, participate in the conversation and advocate for change.

## Business issues

Tackling business issues to support women relates to two key issues – first, around business strategy, and second, the impact of business decision-making on consumers and society more broadly.

Business owners, directors and entrepreneurs, as well as decision-making employees, leaders, and managers, must consider strategies around empowering women, and treating their female employees fairly.

We believe business plans must consider all consumers and develop strategies and products to support women and families. Where possible, an empowerment fund for women in minorities, or difficult environments, can be a great way for organisations to support women in needs.

We also believe that organisations must consider organisational policies and strategies that consider women and non-binary employees. This means consideration of family-friendly policies, flexibility in employment and advancement opportunities for women who choose to advance in their careers. By considering strategies for inclusion for women. For some organisations and industries, particularly those that are overly male dominated, this may mean the introduction of quotas, however quotas don't always work. Instead, ensuring a balanced leadership model with females represented, calling on female experts to support decision-making (not at the exclusion of men, but to ensure a balanced perspective) and ensuring both females and males are included in recruitment decision-making.

Furthermore, diversity training and representation of minorities in key decision-making will support and empower employees and allow them to be 'seen' in corporate strategic decisions.

## Household issues

Our minds draw back to the great women who've gone before us, the ones we learned about in ancient history. Women of the 1500s like Bess of Hardwick, Countess of Shrewsbury, who, through a series of clever marriages and good choices, rose from a modest family to become one of Elizabethan England's wealthiest women, building, and renovating, the enormous Hardwick Hall in Derbyshire. Women of the 1600s like Aphra Behn, a playwright, author, translator and poet who, in Restoration England, was one of the first women to earn a living by writing. Other Stuart era women, like Margaret Cavendish, the Duchess of Newcastle, who while incredibly privileged, still experienced discrimination, even in famously 'liberal' Stuart times where women were given more freedom than ever before. Cavendish's work was wild as well as wildly feminine, for example, she wrote a theory of atomics in a poetic cadence and criticised the invention of the microscope as too masculine and concerned with the world that could not be seen, rather than the world that could. She was obviously a feminist, before such a term even existed and was said to have dressed outrageously, to have sworn prolifically and liberally and to have been described as "mad, conceited and ridiculous". But, it equally goes back to all those women who come before us and who wanted to write but couldn't. The Shakespeare's sisters who are all our sisters who could have done anything, if they'd just had the room to do it in.

The decision to try to juggle it all is ours and ours alone. But, we don't expect men to need to make the same choices. Men's wages increase when they become fathers, but women's wages drop (Kleven, Landais & Søgaard, 2019). Kleven, Landais, and Søgaard (2019) in their research suggest the gender pay gap is basically a motherhood penalty of a price for having children. Men are not subjected to the same cultural and social expectations to care, or to take time off for family as social and cultural pressure dictates to women. They are also not given those stickers that say 'boys can do anything' because the cultural and social expectation is that they will be able to do anything, after all, they're boys.

We have it in our power to change it. We can take it in our own hands to fight the system, or not. There is no reason a woman choosing not to have it all should be criticised any more than a woman who chooses to try to have as much as she can, should be criticised. Those women who are content with their situation, and don't try to do too much should be just as equally respected as those who try to strive to have a career and a life as well. This dichotomy is the problem of modern, early twentieth-century women's experiences. That we are damned if we do and damned if we don't. We hope women reading this book know, we support you and your choices, whatever those choices are. It's not up to anyone, least of all us, to judge your choices.

## Reference list

Bagri, N. T. (2017, January 12). New research confirms the "sexuality pay gap" is real. *Quartz magazine.* Retrieved from https://qz.com/881303/eight-million-americans-are-affected-by-a-pay-gap-that-no-one-talks-about/.

De Maio, J., Silbert, M., Stathopoulos, M., Rioseco, P., Jenkinson, R., & Edwards, B. (2017). *Empowering migrant and refugee women: Supporting and empowering women beyond five-year post-settlement.* Melbourne, Australia: Australian Institute of Family Studies.

Fric, K. (2019). How does being out at work relate to discrimination and unemployment of gays and lesbians? *Journal for Labour Market Research, 53*(1), 1–19.

Johns, R. (2021) University of Canberra indigenous student research report: Recruitment, retention and success recommendations, Report. Australia: University of Canberra

Kleven, H., Landais, C., & Søgaard, J. E. (2019). Children and gender inequality: Evidence from Denmark. *American Economic Journal: Applied Economics, 11*(4), 181–209.

Loh, M.I., & Klug, J. (2012). Voices of migrant women: The mediating role of resilience on the relationship between acculturation and psychological distress. *The Australian Community Psychologist, 24*, 59–78.

SNAICC (National Voice for our Children) (2020). The family matters report 2020: Measuring trends to turn the tide on the over-representation of Aboriginal and Torres Strait Islander children in out-of-home care in Australia. Retrieved from https://www.familymatters.org.au/wp-content/uploads/2020/11/FamilyMattersReport2020_LR.pdf?mc_cid=38b1093983&mc_eid=571fa80e1b.

Ziwica, K. (2021, July 10–16). The case that may close the wage gap. *The Saturday Paper.* Retrieved from https://www.thesaturdaypaper.com.au/news/politics/2021/07/10/the-case-that-might-close-the-wage-gap/162583920012035.

# Index

Note: **Bold** page numbers refer to tables and *italic* page numbers refer to figures.

For Product Safety Concerns and Information please contact our EU
representative GPSR@taylorandfrancis.com
Taylor & Francis Verlag GmbH, Kaufingerstraße 24, 80331 München, Germany